Praise for *Teaching Better*

"*Written by two teachers who experienced lesson study while they taught in Japan, this well-written book makes an important contribution to our understanding of lesson study and instructional improvement more broadly. Compelling case studies bring to life the process of collaborative inquiry. Teachers, coaches, and school and district administrators will find useful tools to grow and support school-wide inquiry-based improvement.*"

—Catherine Lewis
Distinguished Research Scholar
Mills College
Oakland, CA

"*Through compelling images, metaphors, and insights from their research in Japan and the United States, Bradley Ermeling and Genevieve Graff-Ermeling vividly remind us that learning to teach well is an ongoing journey for the long haul. This powerful book is a must-read for teachers and leaders who embrace the idea of deep and continuous instructional improvement and want to know how to realize it in their schools.*"

—Margaret Heritage
Senior Scientist
WestEd
San Francisco, CA

"*Teaching Better is a compelling and detailed account of the 'talk,' interactions, and work products that characterize substantive improvement activities. A significant contribution to the work of improvement science.*"

—Ronald Gallimore
Distinguished Professor Emeritus
University of California, Los Angeles
Los Angeles, CA

"*For those policymakers, administrators, and practitioners considering how to improve instruction through teacher collaboration, read* Teaching Better. *Filled with case studies, the book has an undentable rationale and clear road map for teachers to work together.*"

—Larry Cuban
Professor Emeritus
Stanford University Graduate School of Education
Palo Alto, CA

Teaching Better

To the many educators who inspired this book through their faithful commitment to teaching better.

Teaching Better

Igniting and Sustaining Instructional Improvement

Bradley A. Ermeling
Genevieve Graff-Ermeling

A Joint Publication

CORWIN
A SAGE Publishing Company

learningforward
THE PROFESSIONAL LEARNING ASSOCIATION

FOR INFORMATION:

Corwin

A SAGE Company

2455 Teller Road

Thousand Oaks, California 91320

www.corwin.com

SAGE Publications Ltd.

1 Oliver's Yard

55 City Road

London, EC1Y 1SP

United Kingdom

SAGE Pvt. Ltd.

B 1/I 1 Mohan Cooperative Industrial Area

Mathura Road, New Delhi 110 044

India

SAGE Publications Asia-Pacific Pte. Ltd.

3 Church Street

#10-04 Samsung Hub

Singapore 049483

Printed in the United States of America

Library of Congress Cataloging-in-Publication Data

Names: Ermeling, Bradley A., author. | Graff-Ermeling, Genevieve, author.

Title: Teaching better : igniting and sustaining instructional improvement / Brad Ermeling, Genevieve Graff-Ermeling.

Description: Thousand Oaks, California : Corwin, a SAGE Company, [2016] | Includes bibliographical references and index.

Identifiers: LCCN 2015042091 | ISBN 9781506333465 (pbk. : alk. paper)

Subjects: LCSH: Effective teaching. | Reflective teaching.

Classification: LCC LB1025.3 .E76 2016 | DDC 371.102—dc23 LC record available at http://lccn.loc.gov/2015042091

This book is printed on acid-free paper.

Program Director: Dan Alpert

Senior Associate Editor: Kimberly Greenberg

Editorial Assistant: Katie Crilley

Production Editor: Veronica Stapleton Hooper

Copy Editor: Pam Schroeder

Typesetter: C&M Digitals (P) Ltd.

Proofreader: Ellen Howard

Cover Designer: Rose Storey

Marketing Manager: Charline Maher

Certified Chain of Custody
Promoting Sustainable Forestry
www.sfiprogram.org
SFI-01268

SFI label applies to text stock

16 17 18 19 20 10 9 8 7 6 5 4 3 2 1

Contents ●—

List of Improvement Portraits   x

List of Companion Website Content   xi

Foreword   xii
    Ronald Gallimore

Acknowledgments   xvi

About the Authors   xvii

About the Artists   xix

Introduction   1

  A Vision for Teaching Better   1
  Depth and Detail Lost in Translation   2
  Reframing Instructional Improvement   2
  Integrating Portraits, Principles, and Stories   4
  Practitioner Resources and Context for Use   6
  Who Should Read This Book?   6
  The Continuous Pursuit   7

**Chapter 1 • One Plank at a Time: The Steady
Discipline of Instructional Improvement**   10

  Lessons Learned From a Chalkboard   13
  Comparing U.S. and Japanese Approaches   16
  Conclusion   17

**Chapter 2 • Learning to Learn From Teaching:
A Firsthand Account of Lesson Study
in Japan**   22

  Background on Lesson Study   23
  Project Context   25
  Author Roles and Project Timeline   25
  Teachers' Room: Home Base for Lesson Study Planning   25
  Selection of Research Theme   27
  Planning the Research Lesson   27
  Within-School Research Lesson and Reflection Meeting   30
  Lessons Revisions   30

Public Research Lesson and Reflection Meeting   36
Final Reflections From the English Team   38
Insights Gained From Our Apprenticeship: Essential
    Skills and Mindsets   39
Conclusion   45

**Chapter 3 • Expanding Horizons: A Case Study
of U.S. Teachers Collaborating to
Change Practice**   **50**

Lesson Study Comes to a U.S. High School   53
Video-Based Lesson Observations   55
Project Phases and Time   55
Identifying a Research Theme   55
Developing a Working Hypothesis   57
Round 1: Uneven Attempts   59
Round 2: A Breakthrough in Productive Struggle   65
Final Reflections   71
Conditions That Enabled Collaborative Improvement   72
Conclusion   80

**Chapter 4 • Deepening Knowledge: Why
Expansive Change Is Difficult and
What We Might Do About It**   **84**

Why Expansive Change Is So Difficult   86
Addressing the Problem   87
Conclusion   101

**Chapter 5 • Matching Vision With Resources:
A Reconceived Model for Leadership
and Assistance**   **106**

Traditional Patterns of Assistance   108
Strategically Assisting Performance   109
Conclusion   127

**Chapter 6 • Multiplying Power: How Joint
Productive Activity Revived Two
Problematic Teams**   **130**

Story #1: Focusing on Successful Action   133
Story #2: Finding Common Ground   136
Key Principles for Reviving Problematic Teams   140
Conclusion   143

Chapter 7 • Remaining Stubborn for a
Long Time: Six Practitioner Stories
of Courage and Persistence   **146**

Paula Fernandez—Special Education Teacher   149
Maria Alvarez—English as a Second Language Teacher 150
Tom Richards—Science Teacher   153
Doug Wilson—Math Teacher   154
John Wooden—Basketball Teacher   157
Hank Bias—Basketball Teacher   158
Back to the Track   160

Appendix: Leader's Guide to Improvement Portraits   163

Glossary: Japanese Words and Phrases   172

Index   174

List of Improvement Portraits

Portrait #1: Rotting Ship at Sea
Artistic Image   10
Metaphor Description   12

Portrait #2: Rich Drop of Food Coloring
Artistic Image   22
Metaphor Description   24

Portrait #3: Japanese Toothpick *(Tsumayōji)*
Artistic Image   50
Metaphor Description   51

Portrait #4: Virtual Treasure Chest
Artistic Image   84
Metaphor Description   93

Portrait #5: Winter Horseshoes
Artistic Image   106
Metaphor Description   107

Portrait #6: Joint Productive Activity (JPA)
Artistic Image   130
Metaphor Description   131

Portrait #7: 5000 Reasons to Quit
Artistic Image   146
Metaphor Description   147

List of Companion •━━
Website Content

  http://www.corwin.com/ErmelingTeachingBetter

Improvement Portrait Resources
Presentation Slides With Full-Color Digital Images
Presentation Ideas and Metaphor Descriptions

Japanese Words and Audio
Japanese Glossary With Audio Clips for Correct Pronunciation

Application Resources

Chapter 1
Balancing Urgency and Intentionality Reflection Exercise

Chapter 2
Essential Skills and Mindsets Reflection Exercise

Chapter 3
Collaborative Improvement Reflection Exercise
Pilot Team Selection Inventory
Protocol Criteria Checklist

Chapter 4
Teaching Discovery Reflection Exercise

Chapter 5
Winter Horseshoes Reflection Exercise
Triadic Model Exercise
Organizing Settings Template
Assistance Matrix Exercise
Assistance Matrix Template
KTL Summary Pilot Exercise

Chapter 6
Reviving Problematic Groups Reflection Exercise

Chapter 7
Courage and Persistence Reflection Exercise
Suggestions for Conducting Individual Inquiry With a Mentor

Better Teaching: A Long Voyage on an Infinite Sea

··

Teaching Better confronts American education's addiction to quick-fix solutions: that sad, familiar, and self-defeating cycle of reforms launched with soaring aspirations only to land on the shoals of little achieved—quickly followed by another hopeful reform ending in disappointing wreckage.

This self-defeating cycle never allows time for the teaching improvements to be fully implemented. Reforms are painted in broad brush strokes that must be translated into instructional details by teachers—teachers inquiring, planning, trying out, and revising hundreds of lessons. Progress is always uneven when seeking change, often slower than anticipated, and commonly running afoul of "hurry-up" pressures that sink reforms before they are completed.

The authors have a broader, more radical vision of seeking better teaching. They cast it as fundamental to the profession: a career-long commitment to continuous improvement promising deep satisfaction and personal pride.

Brad and Genevieve are teachers; they know the explanatory power of metaphors. They liken the search for better teaching to a long "voyage of discovery into unknown lands, seeking not for new territory but for new knowledge. It should appeal to those with a good sense of adventure" (Nobelprize.org, n.d., para. 3).

They visualize teachers as sailors sailing a rotting ship on an infinite sea. There are no ports—repairs must be made under way. Doing nothing or hasty repair courts disaster. Pressure and stress are constants.

To save the ship, the crew must collaborate in the "midst of tumultuous waves, internal disagreement, and unpredictable obstacles" (this volume, p. 17). They must balance urgency to address imminent problems with "patience and discipline to investigate 'one plank at a time'" (this volume, p. 10).

> As crew members and sailors on the ship, school leaders and
> teachers are faced with the challenge of collaboratively rebuilding
> and modifying their practice at just the right increments while
> balancing competing concerns. They are simultaneously responsible
> for redressing serious gaps in teaching and learning while also
> staying on course and navigating a demanding curriculum. There
> is no option for placing school on hold for six months, docking the
> ship, and restarting again in the spring. (this volume, p. 13).

Sadly, the addiction to quick fixes often leads to hasty efforts to implement
major changes in districts and schools. For example, Chapter 1 describes
a presentation to a group of regional superintendents when Brad and
several University of California Los Angeles (UCLA) colleagues shared
research findings on effective processes for instructional improvement.
One superintendent asked how long it would take for such a model to
yield achievement results across the district.

> Hearing it would take at least five to seven years and likely much
> longer, the group responded with dismay. A few superintendents
> laughed and one district representative said, "We can't wait
> that long. Is there a way we can move this faster?" (this volume,
> p. 11).

Thoroughly addicted to quick fixes, often enabled by local political
pressures, too many schools and districts roll out new programs across all
grades in one year. The results are predictable. The addiction to quick fixes
in American education floats on, untouched as a sailboat bobbing gently in
a warm tropical lagoon. The addicted will take no comfort from this book.
But rehabilitation is possible for those open to change.

The first step is admitting to addiction. Brad and Genevieve make a case
that quick-fix, distant-from-practice professional development can no
longer be the go-to form of instructional improvement. For teaching
to get better, teachers need to regard themselves and to be regarded as
permanent learners with dedicated time to inquire, develop, try out, and
refine their teaching—*teacher inquiry* is the term they use to describe this
iterative process of improving instruction.

Among the most productive forms of inquiry, they argue, are peer
collaborations. Collaborations are most successful when schools provide
stable, protected settings for facilitated study of teaching. If teacher

collaboration and inquiry are afterthoughts and "if we have time" activities, or their settings are hijacked for other purposes, not much is accomplished.

Collaborative inquiry has to become part of the daily routine of work and be supported by administrators to hold everyone accountable for pursuing better teaching. Because better teaching is the key to any goal of importance—student achievement for example—what activity should have a higher priority for teachers and administrators?

The book illustrates, through detailed story and metaphor, the value of systematic and collaborative inquiry—infused with knowledge and support—as a course to better teaching. It offers compelling and detailed illustrations of "talk," interactions, and work products that characterize substantive improvement activities. Drawing on firsthand experience from both the United States and Japan, Brad and Genevieve offer multiple examples of the power and potential of sustained, focused inquiry conducted by collaborative teacher teams. In Japan it is called *lesson study*, a practice embedded in teachers' school lives and a staple professional development process.

Analogous programs in the United States are now many in name—for example, learning teams, professional learning communities, teacher collaboration, teachers as researchers, and even lesson study—but are rarely implemented with the depth and quality they pretend to advocate. "Instead they function as buzzwords that conceal the depth and promise of powerful improvement activities" (this volume, p. 2). Unlike Japan, there is no standard practice of collaborative inquiry in the United States, and as this book documents, many versions do not provide teachers with useful opportunities to pursue better teaching.

It's easy to claim, "improving teaching is a long voyage that requires sustained collaborative inquiry," but Brad and Genevieve take it a step further. They provide rich, detailed accounts of what confronts educators undertaking inquiry—the challenges and the rewards, the crashing waves and the breathtaking views—accounts based on personal experience with collaborative inquiry in Japan for seven years and in the United States for many more. During these years, they learned to cultivate inquiry skills and mindsets and incrementally test out local adaptations. They learned that teaching is a cultural activity and that "seeing something different" can "create circumstances for change" (this volume, p. 50). And they learned that bold visions of improvement require an equal investment in systems of support.

This richly documented exploration of structures and processes supporting the pursuit of better teaching concludes with six moving stories—stories of teachers that highlight ineffable qualities that underpin a career-long commitment to the continuous improvement of teaching: qualities, such as courage, conviction, and relentlessness, that are sometimes underplayed in books like this and qualities that in turn are strengthened by continuous, productive teacher collaborations and inquiry.

For teachers, and especially those entering and new to the profession, Brad and Genevieve offer a vision that is at once inspirational and daunting: educators steering a ship under constant repair on an infinite sea, navigating toward better teaching against powerful currents and shifting winds.

The navigators are collaborative teacher teams with inquiry as their instrument of navigation.

Every generation of teacher navigators, every new crew, must relentlessly heed the call to duty—plotting new courses to better teaching.

The voyage to better teaching is neither easy nor short. It is a journey without a final port of call.

Brad and Genevieve promise it is trying at times even for the hardiest, but a voyage undertaken and continued leads to riches of spirit and life.

> There is a tide in the affairs of men, Which taken at the flood, leads on to fortune. Omitted, all the voyage of their life is bound in shallows and in miseries. On such a full sea are we now afloat. And we must take the current when it serves, or lose our ventures. (Shakespeare, 1974/1699)

Ronald Gallimore
University of California, Los Angeles

References

Nobelprize.org. (n.d.). Frederick Sanger's speech at the Nobel banquet, December 10, 1980. Retrieved from http://www.nobelprize.org/nobel_prizes/chemistry/laureates/1980/sanger-speech.html

Shakespeare, W. (1974). *Julius Caesar*. In G. B. Evans, et al. (Eds.), *The riverside Shakespeare*. Boston, MA: Houghton Mifflin. (Original work published 1699)

Acknowledgments

O ur sincere thanks to the students, colleagues, mentors, and teachers who have invested in our journey. To all the educators we have learned from and partnered with, and who allowed us to help them grow, thank you for inspiring us to teach better.

Special thanks to our colleagues in Japan who helped us adapt to a new culture and learn to expand our horizons; and to the student artists for their rich depictions of the metaphors—bringing each of them to life.

To Dan Alpert, our editor at Corwin, for seeing so clearly the potential of the book and bringing our ideas into full color. Thanks also to Kimberly Greenberg, Katie Crilley, and our reviewers whose thoughtful contributions greatly enhanced the final product.

To our parents, Vern, Kathy, Paul, and Marilyn, who faithfully taught us Scripture and that in Christ we are redeemed children of God, free to open up the gifts He's given us. And to Ron Gallimore, a mentor and friend whose candid advice, instructive feedback, and probing questions have added our names to the long list of minds he's roused to life.

Publisher's Acknowledgments

Corwin gratefully acknowledges the contributions of the following individuals:

Janice Bradley
School Improvement Specialist
Utah Education Policy Center
University of Utah
Salt Lake City, UT

Tonya Ward Singer
Corwin Author
Independent Consultant
Santa Rosa, CA

Karla J. McAdam
District School Improvement
Coordinator
Decatur Public Schools
Decatur, IL

About the Authors

Photograph by Lomeli Photography

Bradley A. Ermeling is a principal research scientist with Pearson's Research and Innovation Network and a member of a research team from UCLA and Stanford. He spent seven years working as an educator in Japan, developing firsthand knowledge and expertise with Japanese lesson study, and has published numerous articles on developing and supporting systems for collaborative inquiry and continuous learning. In the United States, he taught high school English, special education, and directed professional learning programs before shifting his attention to educational research. He was a corecipient of the 2010 Best Research Award from Learning Forward for his contributions to research on instructional improvement through inquiry teams. He was also coauthor for the article titled "Learning to Learn From Teaching: A Firsthand Account of Lesson Study in Japan," which was named 2015 Outstanding Paper of the Year by Emerald Publishing and the World Association of Lesson Studies. Dr. Brad Ermeling's current research interests include lesson study and collaborative inquiry, facilitation practices that promote productive struggle, and digital resources that support the study of teaching and learning.

Photograph by Lomeli Photography

Genevieve Graff-Ermeling is chief academic officer at Orange Lutheran High School, educational researcher, and consultant. She spent seven years working as an educator in Japan, developing curriculum and participating firsthand in Japanese lesson study projects. She also taught and designed curriculum at the high school level in the United States. She has held several positions as an external coach and site-based facilitator of teacher reflection, design of assessments, inquiry-based science teaching, and the use of data to inform teaching in multiple subject areas for both elementary and secondary, public and private schools. She has a degree in behavioral science with an emphasis in anthropology and helped lead a medical outreach team conducting research in Honduras. She was coauthor of the autoethnography titled, "Learning to Learn From Teaching: A Firsthand Account of Lesson Study in Japan," which was named 2015 Outstanding Paper of the Year by Emerald Publishing and the World Association of Lesson Studies. She was also an elite runner, National Association of Intercollegiate Athletes (NAIA) national champion, and competed in the 5000 meters for the 2004 U.S. Olympic Trials. Genevieve Ermeling's current research interests are practice-based professional learning for high school educators, transformative models of teacher professional growth, and methods for assessing and assisting learning through the zone of proximal development.

Connect With Brad and Genevieve on Twitter

@BradErmeling

@Graff_Ermeling

Use #TeachingBetter to join the conversation.

About the Artists ●———

Joshua Autrey was a student in Brad's high school English class from 2004 to 2005. He is now an engineer in the service department for Ellison Technologies, specializing in five-axis machining. His artwork focuses on realism using all different media. He draws inspiration from industrial, and structural, design. Joshua's 2005 pencil drawing of the "Rotting Ship at Sea" is featured in Chapter 1.

Chelsea Madden was a member of the cross-country program Genevieve coached from 2013 to 2014. She is now an undergraduate student pursuing a degree in mechanical engineering and a minor in fine arts at Baylor University. Chelsea's artwork focuses on a realistic style with her favorite mediums being watercolor, charcoal, and acrylic. She draws inspiration from the human figure and from the world around her. Chelsea's illustrations of the "Rich Drop of Food Coloring" (2013), the "Japanese Toothpick," the "Winter Horseshoes," "Joint Productive Activity," and "5000 Reasons to Quit" (2015) are featured in Chapters 2, 3, 5, 6, and 7.

Emily Tam is a student at Faith Lutheran High School in Las Vegas, Nevada, and a member of the technical theatre and visual arts programs in the Faith Conservatory of the Fine Arts. Her artwork focuses on surrealism and manipulated form, using all mediums to create two- and three-dimensional pieces. She draws inspiration from literature, pop culture, and other artists. Emily's 2015 drawing of the "Virtual Treasure Chest" is featured in Chapter 4.

Introduction •———

S omething unfortunate happens to U.S. teachers when they join the profession. They encounter a culture that forgets teachers are also learners. They enter a world consumed by results and disinterested in process. They join communities that celebrate exemplars and disguise imperfections. They spend long hours in isolated classrooms with minimal time for collaboration or observation. They work in systems that evaluate compliance rather than assist performance. They inherit values and routines that stymie professional growth and discourage continuous improvement.

Working under these conditions, the majority of teachers in U.S. schools have carried out the pursuit of improvement in isolation, without much intentional support or systematic process of study. Faced with the perfect storm of multiple responsibilities and limited time, teachers work through daily cycles of teaching—planning, implementing, and making adjustments as needed—but rarely have opportunities to pause and reflect, or articulate findings about instructional practice. As a result, most teachers acquire knowledge about practice through sporadic moments of reflection in the midst of frenzied daily routines.

A Vision for Teaching Better

What if instead of individuals working on improvement in isolation, the familiar teaching cycle became a joint activity? What if teachers deliberately and continually pursued instructional improvement goals in a focused, collaborative context alongside colleagues who shared the same needs, concerns, and aspirations for *teaching better?* Examples such as Japanese *lesson study* and other carefully designed models of *collaborative instructional inquiry* provide convincing evidence that such an approach can change teaching and improve achievement (Gallimore, Ermeling, Saunders, & Goldenberg, 2009; Lewis, Perry, Friedkin, & Roth, 2012; Perry & Lewis, 2011; Saunders, Goldenberg, & Gallimore, 2009; Weinbaum et al., 2004). National organizations such as the Council of Chief State School Officers (2013), Learning Forward (2011), and the National Commission on Teaching and America's Future (Carroll, Fulton, & Doerr, 2010), have also emphasized ongoing, job-embedded, reflective practice in their recommendations and standards for professional learning. And numerous authors have outlined essential practices for professional learning communities and continuous professional development (e.g., Lieberman & Miller, 2008; McLaughlin & Talbert, 2006).

Depth and Detail Lost in Translation

Growing interest in continuous improvement is a hopeful sign of shifting policy and priorities, but maintaining depth and quality with local implementation is proving difficult to achieve. Many schools and districts have adopted superficial aspects of these ideas, but at a deep level of school culture, they remain devalued and misunderstood. Terms such as *reflective practice*, *lesson study*, and *collaborative inquiry* are in popular use, but their underlying concepts and processes remain so loosely defined and broadly interpreted that they rarely produce intended results. Instead, they function as buzzwords that conceal the depth and promise of powerful improvement activities. In dozens of schools we visited across the nation, we observed teachers engaged in collaborative settings, but their efforts were constrained by hasty implementation, enduring cultural scripts, poorly defined processes, and insufficient support. We watched administrators and teacher leaders struggle, without guidance and resources, to translate the promise of lesson study and collaborative inquiry into concrete, effective action.

Reframing Instructional Improvement

This book provides a series of rich artistic images, instructive metaphors, and detailed examples of collaborative instructional inquiry in action by real teachers, in real schools, facing real problems. It also provides practical resources and specific strategies to help school leaders nurture and sustain instructional improvement. The content is organized around seven inspirational portraits (symbolic images and metaphors) that further define and clarify the steady, continuous work of improving teaching. Each chapter leads off with a high school student's artistic representation of the "improvement portrait" followed by a corresponding key principle that serves as the focal point for the chapter (see Table 1). Symbolically enhanced through the artwork, these images and metaphors help to *reframe* educators' understanding of collaborative inquiry and illuminate important details for what that work can and should look like.

Later in each chapter, a corresponding key segment of text (typically one to two pages) provides a detailed description of the portrait's symbolism and meaning as it relates to the chapter's content. Each description is strategically placed at different points in the chapter narrative, depending on

■ Table 1: Improvement Portraits and Key Principles

Portrait #1: **Rotting Ship at Sea** *Key Principle:* Systematic improvement requires a balance of urgency and intentionality: urgency to pursue and resolve compelling problems but patience and discipline to investigate one plank at a time.	
Portrait #2: **Rich Drop of Food Coloring** *Key Principle:* Steady, concentrated effort over time produces a rich, permeating, and lasting effect.	
Portrait #3: **Japanese Toothpick *(Tsumayōji)*** *Key Principle:* "Seeing that something can be completely different is one of the most effective ways of opening eyes to the ubiquity of cultural practices and creating the circumstances for change" (Gallimore & Stigler, 2003, p. 27).	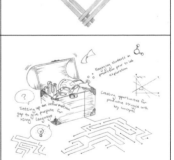
Portrait #4: **Virtual Treasure Chest** *Key Principle:* Hard-won assets of local knowledge should be diligently pursued, continually refined, and globally shared.	
Portrait #5: **Winter Horseshoes** *Key Principle:* Investments in bold ideas should be matched by an equal investment in support and attention to detail.	

(Continued)

■ **Table 1: (Continued)**

Portrait #6: **Joint Productive Activity (JPA)** *Key Principle:* Power is multiplied to the fullest extent when we work together productively.	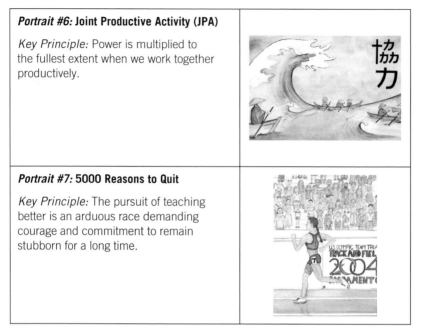
Portrait #7: **5000 Reasons to Quit** *Key Principle:* The pursuit of teaching better is an arduous race demanding courage and commitment to remain stubborn for a long time.	

whether the portrait is better understood when preceded by other narrative content or as a backdrop for subsequent content and ideas.

Integrating Portraits, Principles, and Stories

Each of these *improvement portraits* is combined with detailed implementation stories from our K–12 research and experience in both Japan and the United States. These case studies and stories bring the images to life through unfolding narrative and concrete application of the key principles.

The first half of the book (Chapters 1–3) draws heavily on our extended research and experience with Japanese lesson study, featuring our firsthand accounts from Japan and a detailed case study of U.S. teachers working to adopt the Japanese model. The stories and examples in these chapters provide a clear, alternative image of collaborative instructional inquiry from a culture with a rich history and deeply established system for steady, instructional change. As we quote in Chapter 3, "Seeing that something can be completely different is one of the most effective ways of opening eyes to the ubiquity of cultural practices and creating the circumstances for change" (Gallimore & Stigler, 2003, p. 27).

Chapter 1 includes short anecdotes of purposeful technology integration from 17 videotaped lessons and interviews we conducted in Japanese classrooms. Building on these anecdotes, it presents the case for slow, steady, incremental improvement and the need to balance urgency with intentionality.

Chapter 2 is a firsthand account of our experience as U.S. educators immersed in lesson study at a Japanese school. Drawing on this unique, inside perspective, it describes the critical skills and mindsets required to study and learn from teaching.

Chapter 3 expands on these examples from Japan with a detailed case study of veteran U.S. teachers engaged in a successful science lesson study project. It carefully traces the implementation efforts of each participant and describes the conditions that enabled teachers to make significant changes in practice.

The second half of the book (Chapters 4–7) features a broad range of U.S. examples from different inquiry contexts. These chapters focus on overcoming the challenges and constraints of engaging in collaborative inquiry and highlight specific guidance and strategies for sustaining improvement efforts.

Chapter 4 opens with research observations from a middle school algebra team that struggled to adopt new methods for conceptual teaching. It explains why expansive changes in teaching are difficult to scale, cautions against emphasis on "best practices," and highlights the potential of inquiry-based digital libraries for stimulating growth in knowledge and judgment. It also includes an example of a high school algebra team that used video resources from a digital library to study and implement a more conceptual lesson approach.

Chapter 5 presents a detailed explanation of strategies school leaders can employ to nurture and sustain school-wide collaborative inquiry. It includes a reconceived framework for leadership and assistance, practical tools for organizing settings and distributing support, and concrete suggestions for coauthoring narratives that help teachers reflect on their practice.

Chapter 6 illustrates the power of JPA through two stories of teams (a cross-curricular middle school team and a world language team) that used focused, collaborative inquiry to overcome complex group dynamics and a history of unproductive meetings. Both teams revived their collaborative settings by making a commitment to shared learning goals and refocusing meetings on structured cycles of planning, teaching, and analysis.

Chapter 7 concludes with six compelling vignettes of teachers (special education, English as a second language, math, science, and two coaches) who inspired others through their courageous commitment to teaching, unwavering compassion for students, and enduring focus on improvement.

With the exception of the last two stories in Chapter 7, all school and teacher names in the book have been replaced with pseudonyms.

Practitioner Resources and Context for Use

This book is not limited to a particular inquiry program or model but is designed to support any collaborative instructional inquiry context. As such, it functions as a unique, stand-alone resource but also a terrific companion resource for any manual, handbook, or text that outlines processes and protocols for the collaborative study of teaching.

While not specifically an implementation guide, the book includes a useful set of practitioner resources to help readers translate the ideas into action, including reflection questions for each chapter and a Leader's Guide (see Appendix) with presentation ideas, facilitation notes, and application exercises for each improvement portrait. Chapters 3 through 6 also include templates and tools for establishing teams, coordinating support, and stimulating growth over time. The companion website features full-color, digital versions of each improvement portrait as well as customizable templates, slides, and resources readers can download and adapt for their specific implementation contexts. While organized in a purposeful sequence and progression, the chapters are also self-contained. They can be strategically selected for group study and discussion or read in any order that the group finds beneficial.

Who Should Read This Book?

The images, stories, and resources presented here are intended for educators across various levels of the system who commonly share a responsibility, commitment, or interest in pursuing the improvement of teaching, or perhaps a desire to reconnect with the passion that sparked initial interest in the profession. This includes school-site leaders who shoulder responsibility for professional learning and instructional improvement; subject-area or grade-level leaders working to engage colleagues in productive collaboration and inquiry; district, county, or state-level administrators supporting curriculum, instruction, and professional growth; professors of education and directors of preservice programs preparing educators for continuous learning throughout their careers; and classroom teachers collaborating with a peer or mentor on individual inquiry projects. While the majority of stories and examples describe middle and high school implementation, the concepts and resources are readily applicable for any K–12 context or grade span.

The set of improvement portraits and corresponding key principles are also relevant and applicable for anyone in a teaching role (director, supervisor, counselor, mentor, coach, therapist, or pastor) who strives to advance the learning and betterment of others.

The Continuous Pursuit

Teaching better implies a perpetual pursuit of improvement. It suggests that we never "arrive" at a point of complete mastery but are continuously and relentlessly in search of enhancing our craft. We hope these portraits and stories will inspire you in that journey . . . to continue, to renew, or perhaps even to begin that pursuit.

REFERENCES

Carroll, T., Fulton, K., & Doerr, H. (2010). *Team up for 21st century teaching and learning: What research and practice reveal about professional learning.* Washington, DC: National Commission on Teaching and America's Future.

Council of Chief State School Officers. (2013). *Interstate Teacher Assessment and Support Consortium (InTASC) model core teaching standards and learning progressions for teachers 1.0.* Washington, DC: Author. Retrieved from http://www.ccsso.org/Documents/2013/2013_INTASC_Learning_Progressions_for_Teachers.pdf

Gallimore, R., Ermeling, B. A., Saunders, W. M., & Goldenberg, C. (2009). Moving the learning of teaching closer to practice: Teacher education implications of school-based inquiry teams. *Elementary School Journal, 109*(5), 537–553.

Gallimore, R., & Stigler, J. (2003). Closing the teaching gap: Assisting teachers to adapt to changing standards and assessments. In C. Richardson (Ed.), *Whither assessment?* (pp. 25–36). London, England: Qualifications and Curriculum Authority.

Learning Forward. (2011). *Standards for professional learning.* Oxford, OH: Author. Retrieved from http://learningforward.org/docs/pdf/standardsreferenceguide.pdf?sfvrsn=0

Lewis, C., Perry, R., Friedkin, S., & Roth, J. (2012, November/December). Improving teaching does improve teachers: Evidence from lesson study. *Journal of Teacher Education, 63*, 368–375.

Lieberman, A., & Miller, L. (2008). *Teachers in professional communities: Improving teaching and learning.* New York, NY: Teachers College Press.

McLaughlin, M. W., & Talbert, J. E. (2006). *Building school-based teacher learning communities: Professional strategies to improve student achievement.* Chicago, IL: University of Chicago Press.

Perry, R., & Lewis, C. (2011). *Improving the mathematical content base of lesson study: Summary of results.* Mills College Lesson Study Group. Retrieved from http://www.lessonresearch.net/IESAbstract10.pdf

Saunders, W., Goldenberg, C., & Gallimore, R. (2009). Increasing achievement by focusing grade-level teams on improving classroom learning: A prospective, quasi-experimental study of Title 1 schools. *American Educational Research Journal, 46*(4), 1006–1033.

Weinbaum, S., Allen, D., Blyther, T., Simon, K., Seidel, S., & Rubin, C. (2004). *Teaching as inquiry: Asking hard questions to improve practice and student achievement.* New York, NY: Teachers College Press.

CHAPTER 1

One Plank at a Time

The Steady Discipline of Instructional Improvement

Rotting Ship at Sea

KEY PRINCIPLE

Systematic improvement requires a balance of urgency and intentionality: urgency to pursue and resolve compelling problems but patience and discipline to investigate one plank at a time.

Several years ago, Brad (first author) and a team of UCLA colleagues presented research findings on instructional improvement to a group of regional superintendents overseeing a large urban school system. After listening intently to the presentation, one superintendent asked how long it would take for an instructional inquiry model to yield tangible achievement results across all the district's schools. Hearing it would take at least five to seven years and likely much longer, the group responded with dismay. A few superintendents laughed, and one district representative said, "We can't wait that long. Is there a way we can move this faster?" We responded, "Have you been satisfied with results over the last decade? What if you began this work 10 years ago and now started to experience steady gains? The next 10 years offer the same challenge and opportunity." The room was silent; a few administrators nodded their heads, but most remained resistant and skeptical.

A few years later, Genevieve (second author) met with a team of school leaders to discuss implementation plans for a teacher-led curriculum development project. She inventoried existing settings, which included several annual pupil-free days and subject-area collaboration meetings scheduled two or three times per month. After factoring in holidays and other special events, she calculated just over 30 hours available per year for teachers to complete the work. Based on these estimates, she explained it would take approximately five years for the school to map out and refine a coherent curriculum plan for each of their courses. The team paused in disbelief. One member said, "Can't we finish that in about six months?" Genevieve explained it could possibly be reduced to three years but only with additional teacher settings dedicated to this work. Either way, accomplishing the project goals would require a sustained, multiyear commitment.

Examples like these are prevalent in districts and schools throughout the United States. Slow, steady, continuous improvement is hard work, requiring significant time, focus, and commitment. But these are tall demands in a system overwhelmed with successive waves of politics and programs aimed at quick results. Absent the patience for a serious improvement agenda, the majority of reform policies and initiatives have relied on new standards, high-stakes assessments, teacher evaluation, and increased accountabilities, with minimal resources devoted to support professional learning. A narrow emphasis on management and control, combined with a culture that celebrates quick wins over complex solutions, has fostered an education system antithetical to steady, continuous improvement. As Hiebert, Gallimore, and Stigler (2002) explain, "The history of American education includes a graveyard of good ideas condemned by pressure for fast results" (p. 13).

This pervasive problem raises important questions: How can schools embrace slow, steady improvement while facing annual accountability pressures and immediate needs of the current student population? How can schools embrace and sustain systematic effort within a culture that focuses on quick solutions, catchy slogans, short sound bites, and latest trends? The answer to these questions lies in the delicate balance between intentionality and urgency. Being systematic requires more than simply easing up on the accelerator. Working with urgency also requires much more than turning up the heat and keeping a frantic pace. This challenge is comparable to the task a crew of sailors must confront while repairing a rotting ship out at sea.

PORTRAIT #1: Rotting Ship at Sea

The rotting ship is a metaphor first conceived by Australian social scientist Otto Neurath (1882–1945) to describe the delicate and steady process of scientific research. The metaphor is equally applicable to anyone engaged in continuous improvement and the pursuit of building knowledge about professional practice. Neurath (1944) explains the metaphor as follows:

> Imagine sailors, who, far out at sea, transform the shape of their clumsy vessel from a more circular to a more fishlike one. They make use of some drifting timber, besides the timber of the old structure, to modify the skeleton and the hull of their vessel. But they cannot put the ship in dock in order to start from scratch. During their work they stay on the old structure and deal with heavy gales and thundering waves. In transforming their ship they take care that dangerous leakages do not occur. A new ship grows out of the old one, step by step—and while they are still building, the sailors may already be thinking of a new structure, and they will not always agree with one another. The whole business will go on in a way that we cannot even anticipate today. That is our fate. (p. 47)

Applying this metaphor to the context of schools, a group of educators might think of their instructional practice as this perpetually deteriorating ship, far out at sea, which is in continuous need of repair or even transformation. As crew members and sailors on the ship, school leaders and teachers are faced with the challenge of collaboratively rebuilding and modifying their practice at just the right increments while balancing competing concerns. They are simultaneously responsible for redressing serious gaps in teaching and learning while also staying on course and navigating a demanding curriculum. There is no option for placing school on hold for six months, docking the ship, and restarting again in the spring.

Managing this complex set of conditions requires diligent and systematic effort to maintain the functionality and navigational capacity of the vessel while focusing attention on one particular weak plank at a time for more serious work and repair. It also requires a well-established set of procedures for working together productively and a clearly specified process for efficiently identifying gaps, choosing the best timber available to fill these gaps, and skillfully replacing each plank. Once repaired, the sailors (or educators) can then rely on the newly restored plank for solid footing as they shift their attention to other weak planks that are threatening the stability of the ship. As Campbell (1988) notes, "the proportion of the planks we are replacing to those we treat as sound must always be small" (p. 363).

This metaphor is provocative, but helping educators strike this shrewd balance between urgency and intentionality also requires concrete illustrations of what systematic "ship repair" can look like in an educational context. Part of the challenge is that terms such as *inquiry, reflection,* and *collaboration* have been popularized in U.S. schools but are quickly assimilated with existing practice and routines without sufficient knowledge of the profound changes needed to adopt these ideas with fidelity. Educators assume "we do that already" and perhaps even write off the ideas as ineffectual.

Because there are few examples of sustained instructional improvement in U.S. schools, it's important to look outside our system and learn from alternative images of practice. Next we provide one concrete example from Japan's purposeful and systematic approach to integrating classroom technologies—an example that clearly illustrates the time and disposition required to engage in collaborative, systematic improvement one plank at a time.

Lessons Learned From a Chalkboard

In the winter of 2014, while observing and recording classroom lessons in Saitama, Japan, we captured 17 lesson videos from various subject areas across 1st to 12th grade. During our observations, we were surprised to hear a sound we had not heard for many years—the sound of chalk. Every classroom we visited was equipped with a large, green chalkboard. There were few computers, few projectors or Smart Boards, and no other visible forms of 21st century technology in most of the classrooms. Japanese colleagues and researchers confirmed this was representative of the average K–12 classroom in Japan. In January 2015, the Tokyo Broadcasting System reported that approximately 75 percent of Japanese classrooms still use chalkboards as the primary medium for presentation of lesson content (Sankyuu, 2015).

Our first reaction was one of astonishment. How could Japan, a society known for its creation of gadgets and highly specialized technological devices, be so far behind in their use of 21st century technology?

As we continued to record lessons, we began to note the masterful way Japanese teachers utilized this "primitive" instructional medium. We also noted how teachers and students alike maintained the chalkboard with consistent and diligent care. Each class assigned one student to serve as the *kokuban kakari* (person in charge of the chalkboard), who ensured it was clean and ready for use prior to the opening bell for each period. Teachers treated each centimeter of this freshly cleaned board as valuable real estate. They wrote in straight lines with clear and precise characters and paused to erase stray marks or rewrite illegible content.

Math and science teachers used large geometric drafting tools as guides to draw perfectly symmetrical diagrams and tables. Language arts and social studies teachers used a variety of chalk colors, each with a consistent meaning and precise purpose related to grammatical terms, literary themes, or systems of government. They used magnetic timers on the board to pace activities and posted magnetic labels of student names to assign work space for whole-class demonstrations. Most importantly, teachers carefully preserved a lesson storyline as they progressed across the board. They added elements in a strategic sequence that helped bring coherence to the lesson and rarely erased content unless they reached a major instructional transition.

Board Writing: An Example of Steady, Systematic Improvement

We also conducted post-observation interviews with teachers to ask about instructional planning and decisions. It turns out Japanese educators possess a unique technical vocabulary for describing chalkboard teaching practices, called *bansho* (board writing) and *bansho keikaku* (board-writing planning). Like many instructional practices in Japan, *bansho* has been studied and refined over a period of years through the use of Japanese lesson study. During a typical lesson study project, teachers conduct research, analyze curriculum, and design a detailed *research lesson* to address a jointly selected investigative theme. One team member teaches the research lesson, while colleagues observe and collect data on student learning. The team then engages in extended discussion of results and potential revisions. After two or more cycles of implementation, the process often culminates with an open house, where guests are invited to observe teaching of the refined lesson plan (Ermeling & Graff-Ermeling, 2014; see Chapter 2 for a more detailed description).

See glossary for a complete list of Japanese words and phrases contained in the book. See the companion website for audio clips with Japanese pronunciation (http://www.corwin.com/ErmelingTeachingBetter).

Yoshida (1999) reports how lower elementary mathematics teachers used lesson study to test and refine *bansho* methods with conceptually rich math problems. For each research lesson, teachers carefully mapped out a chalkboard diagram, including space for whole-class review of previously assigned problems, space for posting the new problem, space dedicated for student presentation of ideas, and space for culminating remarks. More than simply displaying information or solutions, teachers used the chalkboard to summarize, organize, and link a sequence of lesson events to facilitate collective thinking. One teacher explained: "I try to organize the blackboard in such a way that my students and I can see how the lesson progressed and what was talked about during the lesson" (p. 439). Reports are available in Japanese bookstores summarizing key findings from various *bansho* lesson-study projects.

Based on analysis of more than 200 videos from the Trends in International Mathematics and Science Study (TIMSS), Stigler and Hiebert (1999) also describe underlying cultural teaching *scripts* that influence technology choices in different countries. Comparing Japanese and U.S. eighth grade math classrooms, they observed that nearly all Japanese teachers used a chalkboard as the primary visual aid, while many American teachers (at the time of the study) used an overhead projector. More importantly, they point out this was not merely a visual aid preference but represented a fundamental distinction in teaching approaches. American teachers often chose an overhead projector because they conceived of the visual aid as a tool for focusing students' attention on one problem at a time and shaping tasks into manageable steps. Even when they used a chalkboard, they would often erase a problem before starting a new one to maintain student focus on immediate information.

The Japanese math teachers, as Yoshida (1999) also noted, used visual aids for a different reason—to provide a record of problems, solution approaches, and key principles discussed over the course of a lesson. In this way, the chalkboard played an important role in helping students make connections and discover new relationships among mathematical ideas (Stigler & Hiebert, 1999). In addition, other Japanese studies report the green color of the chalkboard can provide a calming benefit for students, enabling concentration more effectively than a white background (Sankyuu, 2015).

For these reasons, Japanese teachers' choice to use a chalkboard instead of an overhead projector (in the 1990s), or instead of computer-based slide presentations (in 2015), is more than simply a delayed reaction to adopt new devices. It reflects a thoughtful decision about which technology might best support particular learning opportunities for students. Similarly, research and development projects, funded by the Japanese government, are now underway, investigating the kinds of learning opportunities and instructional methods best facilitated by new digital technologies (Japanese Ministry of Internal Affairs and Communications [MIC], n.d.).

Comparing U.S. and Japanese Approaches

The more we observed Japanese masterful use of the chalkboard, the more we reflected on technology and continuous improvement approaches in U.S. classrooms. Not only do educators rarely discuss the rationale for which technology might best support a particular learning opportunity, but numerous studies and reports suggest that U.S. schools often make large investments in new technologies without equal investment in thoughtful implementation (Boser, 2013; Cuban, 2003; Gliksman, 2014; Hess, 2006). While many classrooms are decked out with shiny new tablets, document projectors, Smart Boards, or infrared response systems, far too often these devices are underutilized, and methods of use vary widely across teachers. There are definitely exceptions to this pattern, such as Project RED or the Digital Promise League of Innovative Schools, where technology is carefully implemented through ongoing research and development efforts (League Research, n.d.; Project RED: The Research, n.d.). But there are many more classrooms where digital devices function as little more than expensive and colorful accessories with minimal influence on existing instructional methods. In other cases, devices sit unused, collect dust, and soon become obsolete, costing thousands of dollars in upgrades.

Despite Japan's slower pace of technology adoption, one might argue that Japanese educators are well ahead of the United States in *effective* technology integration. Japanese government officials and other prominent educational leaders openly acknowledge the need to begin incorporating 21st century technologies into their teaching and learning environments. Several programs are well under way with this effort, such as the Future Schools Promotion Project, involving systematic research on infrastructure and effectiveness of technology integration in selected Japanese pilot schools (MIC, n.d.).

Passed down over centuries, Japanese educators have a specific term they use that fittingly describes their approach to honing new practices and integrating new innovations. The term, *jikkuri,* signifies a steady, diligent, and tenacious approach to learning that places value on process and avoids setting close, easy goals. Starting in early elementary school, teachers work with students to nurture this mindset of conscientious thinking and persistence. Teachers and administrators also apply this approach to their own professional learning and continuous improvement efforts (M. Ishii, personal communication, May 15, 2015; H. Kuno, personal communication, May 16, 2015; Miyazaki City Board of Education, n.d.).

This explains why the focus in Japanese education is not on how many innovations they rush to implement or how many new gadgets students get to use. Instead, educators focus on collecting evidence of effectiveness and leveraging technology resources (whether it's a chalkboard or a Smart Board) with purpose and intentionality to enhance and facilitate teaching and learning opportunities. The point is not to resist change or avoid new technologies; the point is to be intentional about instructional choices and how they might improve student learning. As stated in a recent Japanese publication from the Future Schools Promotion Project, "Traditional education will be valued while those parts of it that should be extended, broadened, or deepened will evolve significantly" (MIC, n.d., p. 2).

Conclusion

In his rotting ship metaphor, Neurath points out that our fate as lifelong sailors on the ship is one of continuous rebuilding and searching for improvement, sometimes in the midst of tumultuous waves, internal disagreement, and numerous other unpredictable obstacles. But the sailors learn to embrace the work of overcoming these obstacles as part of the journey and shared responsibility of life at sea, which also brings great satisfaction from faithfully executing duties, honing nautical skills, diligently maintaining the ship's structure, and safely reaching each new destination. This is the same approach Japanese educators have demonstrated for decades in their patient, collaborative study of *bansho*.

What if educators adopted this approach in America with devices such as Smart Boards and infrared response systems as well applications such as screencasting, Google Docs, or Evernote? Teams of teachers could treat these devices and applications as critical topics for collaborative inquiry, develop plans for using them in the classroom, articulate hypotheses for how they will create specific learning opportunities, and implement, observe, and collect data on the results of these lessons. Other teachers could build on these lesson cases by studying, adapting, and refining methods of use for various contexts and learning goals.

And what if a process like lesson study was used as the primary mechanism for all continual professional learning and improvement efforts? In the next chapter, we provide a comprehensive account of Japanese lesson study from our own firsthand experience working as educators immersed in a Japanese school. We also describe the significant cognitive and sociocultural adjustments required to participate in the process and highlight essential skills and mindsets for engaging in this work.

REFLECTION QUESTIONS

KEY PRINCIPLE: *Systematic improvement requires a balance of urgency and intentionality: urgency to pursue and resolve compelling problems but patience and discipline to investigate one plank at a time.*

1. How would you describe the balance between urgency and intentionality in your school or district? What are some specific examples?

2. In what ways has pressure for quick results influenced your instructional improvement efforts? Describe any changes you have implemented that suffered from an urgent timeline?

3. What is an example where you implemented a change with intentionality? What helped make that possible?

4. Reflecting on your curriculum and instruction, what are some of the next planks you might prioritize for deliberate study and repair?

ADDITIONAL RESOURCES

- See Leader's Guide in the Appendix for additional team exercises from this chapter and presentation ideas for the "Rotting Ship at Sea" portrait.
- Visit the companion website to download presentation slides, including a full color digital image of the portrait. Also find customizable templates, checklists, and tools to assist your implementation efforts.

Available at http://www.corwin.com/ErmelingTeachingBetter

REFERENCES

Boser, U. (2013). *Are schools getting a big enough bang for their education technology buck?* Retrieved from http://www.americanprogress.org/issues/education/report/2013/06/14/66485/are-schools-getting-a-big-enough-bang-for-their-education-technology-buck/

Campbell, D. T. (1988). Qualitative knowing in action research. In E. S. Overman (Ed.), *Methodology and epistemology for social science: Selected papers of Donald T. Campbell* (pp. 360–376). Chicago, IL: University of Chicago Press.

Cuban, L. (2003). *Oversold and underused: Computers in the classroom.* Cambridge, MA: Harvard University Press.

Ermeling, B.A., & Graff-Ermeling, G. (2014). Learning to learn from teaching: A first-hand account of lesson study in Japan. *International Journal for Lesson and Learning Studies, 3*(2), 170–192. Retrieved from http://independent.academia.edu/BradleyErmeling

Gliksman, S. (2014). The LAUSD iPad initiative: 5 critical technology integration lessons. *Edutopia.* Retrieved from http://www.edutopia.org/blog/lausd-ipad-technology-integration-lessons-sam-gliksman

Hess, F. (2006, March 30). Technically foolish: Why technology has made our public schools less efficient. *Weekly Standard Online.* Retrieved from http://www.aei.org/article/24119

Hiebert, J., Gallimore, R., & Stigler, J. W. (2002). A knowledge base for the teaching profession: What would it look like and how can we get one? *Educational Researcher, 31*(5), 3–15.

Japanese Ministry of Internal Affairs and Communications (MIC). (n.d.). *Creating the learning environment of the future.* Retrieved from http://www.soumu.go.jp/main_content/000299868.pdf

League Research. (n.d.). *Digital promise.* Retrieved from http://www.digitalpromise.org/initiatives/research#league-research

Miyazaki City Board of Education. (n.d.). Math lessons that nurture the joy and satisfaction of learning: Let's strive to teach tightly developed lessons that encourage deliberate learning. Retrieved from http://mkkc.miyazaki-c.ed.jp/jugyo_point/point_sugaku.pdf

Neurath, O. (1944). *Foundations of the social sciences.* Chicago, IL: University of Chicago Press.

Project RED: The Research. (n.d.). In *Project RED: Revolutionizing education.* Retrieved from http://one-to-oneinstitute.org/research-overview

Sankyuu, T. (Presenter). (2015, January 22). Chalk industry crisis: Decision to cease production of long standing educational IT. [Radio Broadcast]. In K. Arakawa (Producer), *Day Catch News Ranking.* Tokyo, Japan: Tokyo Broadcasting System Holdings, Inc.

Stigler, J., & Hiebert, J. (1999). *The teaching gap: Best ideas from the world's teachers for improving education in the classroom.* New York, NY: Free Press.

Yoshida, M. (1999). *Lesson study: An ethnographic investigation of school-based teacher development in Japan.* Retrieved from ProQuest Dissertations and Theses database. (AAT 9951855)

Some portions of this chapter were adapted
from previously published work in the following:

Ermeling, B. A. (2015). Lessons learned from a chalkboard: Slow and steady technology integration. *Teachers College Record.* Retrieved from http://www.tcrecord.org (ID Number: 17931). Adapted with permission of *Teachers College Record,* www.tcrecord.org. All rights reserved.

CHAPTER 2

Learning to Learn From Teaching

A Firsthand Account of Lesson Study in Japan

Rich Drop of Food Coloring

KEY PRINCIPLE

Steady, concentrated effort over time produces a rich, permeating, and lasting effect.

I n February 1994, just six months after completing teacher preparation courses in the United States, we arrived in Saitama prefecture (about 25 miles north of Tokyo) to begin full-time assignments at a Japanese school in Urawa city. A separate elementary, middle, and high school were all uniquely contained within the same building, sharing the same staff and resources. As the only non-Japanese faculty members, we gradually developed fluency with Japanese through evening language classes and national standardized Japanese proficiency exams. Over a period of seven years, we taught oral English communication classes, designed international exchange programs for students, and coordinated professional development and exchange programs for Japanese teachers and U.S. university professors. We also participated regularly in various forms of authentic Japanese lesson study.

Background on Lesson Study

The English term *lesson study* comes from the Japanese words *jugyō kenkyū* as *jugyō* means "lesson" and *kenkyū* means "study" or "research." During a typical lesson study cycle, teachers jointly select a long-term investigative theme, gather available research, study the curriculum, and design a detailed lesson for a selected topic related to the theme. One team member teaches the research lesson (*kenkyū jugyō*), while colleagues observe and collect data on student learning. An extensive discussion follows the observation, focusing on evidence collected and proposed lesson revisions. The team redesigns the instructional plan based on these reflections and chooses a member to reteach the lesson. The process culminates with an open house where additional faculty and guests observe the lesson and collect data on student learning. After a formal debriefing and analysis that includes the guests, teachers reflect on their experience, document findings, and consider questions for subsequent lesson study cycles (Ermeling & Graff-Ermeling, 2014a; Fernandez, Cannon, & Chokshi, 2003; Lewis, 2002; Stigler & Hiebert, 1999).

As a form of instructional inquiry, lesson study is consistent with studies of effective professional learning, which emphasize shared goals, collective responsibility, authentic assessment, self-directed reflection, stable settings, and supportive leadership (e.g., Carroll, Fulton, & Doerr, 2010). In contrast to generic professional development or compliance-driven reforms, lesson study begins in the classroom and focuses on teachers gaining knowledge and making adjustments through collaborative investigation of individual lessons. As Stigler and Hiebert (1999) explain, each lesson holds *ecological validity:* "Even a single lesson retains the key complexities—curriculum, student characteristics, materials, and physical environment . . . that must be taken into account as we try to improve classroom teaching" (p. 122).

PORTRAIT #2: Rich Drop of Food Coloring

Expanding on this description, one powerful image we learned for lesson study was the comparison to a rich drop of food coloring gradually diffusing through a container of water. When an ordinary drop of colorless water is released into the container, there is a momentary ripple effect but no lasting or discernible change in the water's properties or appearance. If multiple drops of ordinary, colorless water are added, the ripple effect lasts a few seconds longer, and the volume of water increases, but there is still no lasting or significant change. By contrast, when a single drop of food coloring is added to the water, there is a deep, pervasive effect that gradually spreads through the entire container and dramatically changes the water to a rich, indelible color.

A comparison of professional learning activities for teachers offers the same contrast of options. Like a container of water consisting of a vast quantity of water molecules, teaching involves an expansive range of knowledge and skills across a broad curriculum of standards and topics. In the United States, training events and activities aimed at helping teachers master this complex responsibility have traditionally focused on sporadic episodes of generic information and ideas that have a short-lived, superficial ripple effect. With little opportunity for collaboration and no deliberate plan for application or follow-up, these events leave teachers with more resources and materials piled up on their shelves or filed away in hard drives but seldom lead to substantial changes or improvements in teaching.

By contrast, the story in this chapter provides an example of a distinctly different approach used by Japanese educators to engage in collaborative, job-embedded reflection and inquiry. This kind of focused investigation requires a steady, concentrated effort on a few key problems and lessons over time. The end result is a deep, pervasive knowledge that diffuses through daily practice and has a lasting effect on decisions about teaching and learning.

Project Context

The term *lesson study* encompasses a wide continuum of reflective practices that share a common feature: the observation and analysis of live classroom research lessons by a group of teachers (Lewis, Perry, & Murata, 2006). In our experience, some observation events were school-wide activities, others were departmental, and some were associated with district-level education research groups (*kyōiku kenkyū kai*). This is consistent with variations of Japanese lesson study described by other researchers (Chichibu & Kihara, 2013; Lewis & Takahashi, 2013). Within-school observation events were called *kōnai kenkyū jugyō* (within-school research lessons); public observation events were referred to as *kōkai kenkyū jugyō* (public research lessons).

Our most formative lesson study experience was in a district-level research group for English teachers. The Japanese school year stretched from April to March, divided by trimesters. Each trimester, one school hosted a research lesson observation for the district. After visiting another junior high school during the first trimester, the research group nominated our school for the second event in late October.

Author Roles and Project Timeline

In the early planning stages, our English department identified the ninth grade oral communication class as the investigative context for this project. Brad taught this course in a team-teaching format, assisted by the Japanese ninth grade teacher responsible for English grammar, reading, and writing classes. Genevieve participated in planning and observation sessions for the research lesson and helped prepare materials for guest observers. Figure 2.1 provides an overview of the project phases, participants, and length of time devoted to each phase.

Teachers' Room: Home Base for Lesson Study Planning

Our daily professional routines in Japan were defined by membership in the school community and a strong sense of reciprocal accountability. Each day began by switching from outdoor to indoor shoes at faculty lockers and proceeding upstairs to the *shokuin shitsu* ("staff room" or "teachers' room"; see Figure 2.2) where all teachers' desks were arranged side by

■ **Figure 2.1: Lesson Study Project Phases, Participants, and Time Estimates**

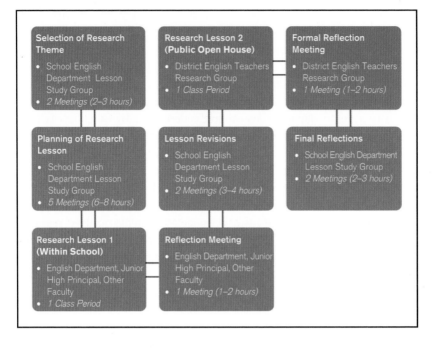

■ **Figure 2.2: Diagram of *Shokuin Shitsu* ("staff room" or "teachers' room")**

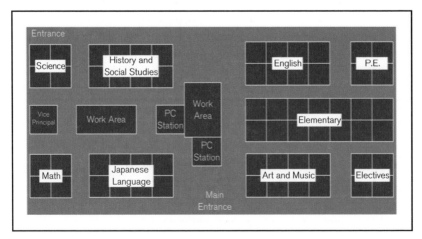

side and grouped by departments. Daily opening and closing meetings took place in the *shokuin shitsu* at 8:05 a.m. and 5:05 p.m. Elementary and middle school teachers spent approximately 22 hours per week in direct classroom teaching; high school teachers spent about 16 hours. Between periods, teachers used the *shokuin shitsu* to collaborate, prepare, grade papers, make phone calls, or meet with students, often returning home after 7:00 p.m. This shared space was also where we planned for lesson study projects.

Selection of Research Theme

In late August, the English department convened two meetings to select a research theme for our school-based lesson study work, which would supplement our participation in the district-level project. After reviewing recent evidence (e.g., student work, classroom observations, survey responses) and discussing the school-wide emphasis on "independence and self-reliance" (*jiritsu*), the group settled on "fostering students' initiative in communication" as the departmental theme for the upcoming lesson study project. Brad and the Japanese team teacher would teach the research lesson on two occasions: once for preliminary within-school observation and a second, revised lesson for formal district-level observation in late October.

Planning the Research Lesson

With this research theme in mind, the English team studied the ninth grade curriculum and the specific unit for October, which focused on building vocabulary and conversation skills for immediate past recreation activities. We designed a specific lesson and dialogue exercise to help students communicate about recent summer vacation experiences. Table 2.1 shows the "Plan to Guide Teaching and Learning," including the research theme, goals, and design rationale. It also includes the evaluation plan and example dialogue exercise.

Building on a rough draft from the Japanese ninth grade teacher, we designed five learning activities as outlined in the *lesson progression* (see non-italicized sections of Table 2.2). After a brief opening greeting, we planned to model the sample dialogue for students, followed by 10 minutes of teacher-supported pair practice and memorization. Each student pair would then perform the dialogue in front of class, concluding with additional pronunciation and intonation practice based on observed patterns of persistent difficulty.

The premise of our design was to create a sequence of activities that scaffolded students' communication abilities, providing a sample dialogue

■ Table 2.1: Plan to Guide Teaching and Learning

Course: 9th Grade Oral Communication

Unit: Communicating About Recreation and Vacation

Lesson Title: What Did You Do This Summer?

Materials: Handouts with example dialogue

Research Theme: Fostering students' initiative in communication

Goals for the Lesson: To verbally communicate and sustain dialogue about immediate past (or recent past) vacation activities

Unit Goals:

1. To build vocabulary for listening and speaking about degrees of pleasure or displeasure (like or dislike) for various recreational activities

Key Vocabulary: not bad, so-so, wonderful, terrific, very disappointing, fantastic, nothing special, pretty boring, awful, really great, all right, terrible

2. To build vocabulary for listening and speaking about vacation activities

Key Vocabulary: went away, stayed home, went to the beach, went to the country, went to xxx, went skiing, hosted relatives, visited relatives

3. To develop skills in listening for gist of a conversation about recreation (the main point or essence), details regarding recreation (what someone did), and attitude toward the experience (pleasure or displeasure)

4. To verbally communicate and sustain dialogue about immediate past (or recent past) recreational or vacation activities

Prior Lessons: Communicating About Food and Restaurants, Engaging in Small Talk

Current Lesson: Communicating About Summer Vacation Activities

Upcoming Lessons: Communicating About Shopping and Movies

Prior Student Knowledge:

Students should be familiar with vocabulary from previous lessons for expressing likes and dislikes with various recreational activities.

Since the lesson takes place in fall, students will have recent memories of summer vacation, and several of the ninth grade students were participants in the school's *beikoku kenshū* (America study) program.

Students will have prior exposure to many familiar words associated with travel and vacation, which are incorporated into the Japanese language through *katakana* (separate Japanese alphabet used specifically for imported foreign words). We will want to anticipate those words (such as Disneyland and California) and help students break habits of resorting to *katakana* pronunciation patterns.

Design Rationale (working hypothesis):

By introducing a sample dialogue structure for informal conversation about recent past events (specifically summer vacation), we hope to foster students' abilities to construct and personalize similar responses and dialogue about their own experiences. The lesson is also based on the premise that memorizing and practicing authentic conversation examples, combined with modeling and pronunciation guidance from a native speaker, might help students gain necessary confidence, vocabulary, and skill to communicate about recent past recreational experiences. This lesson builds on previous lessons and vocabulary for expressing likes and dislikes with various recreational activities as well as restaurant dining experiences. It also paves the way for the upcoming lessons where students will express similar attitudes or impressions regarding shopping and movies.

Evaluation Plan:

Immediate: Teachers will keep notes on a clipboard for each presentation pair regarding pronunciation, intonation, memorization, and delivery (whether students express dialogue with a sense of meaning). These notes are for formative purposes not for official grades.

End of Term: Listening Test with CD-ROM

Example Dialogue:

A: How was your summer?

B: Not bad, but it went by too fast.

A: Did you travel anywhere?

B: Yes. I went to California for a week to visit relatives.

A: What did you do?

B: We spent time at the beach and also went to Disneyland.

A: Did you enjoy the beach?

B: It was all right, but the weather was too hot. I got a terrible sunburn.

A: Did you like the food in America?

B: It was OK. But I missed Japanese food.

structure for future use to formulate and personalize their own responses. We hypothesized that memorizing and practicing authentic conversation examples, combined with modeling and pronunciation guidance from a native speaker, might help students gain necessary confidence, vocabulary, and skill to communicate about recent past recreational experiences.

Since the district observers were English teachers and fluent in both languages, we created an English translation of the standard lesson study template. The detailed format required anticipation of expected student and teacher responses (see Column 2 of Table 2.2). It also required a specific goal and rationale for each lesson segment (see Column 3), specifying how the activity fit into the overall lesson storyline and how it might advance students' ability to initiate and sustain English conversation. The team spent approximately five hours in planning meetings discussing and drafting these notes for the initial research lesson.

Within-School Research Lesson and Reflection Meeting

The school had two classrooms of ninth grade students (9A and 9B). We presented a preliminary within-school research lesson (*kōnai kenkyū jugyō*) to the 9A students, while the English department, junior high principal, and several additional faculty members participated as observers. Each observer received a copy of the lesson plan, equally divided areas of the room to focus attention on a small group of students, and lined the perimeter to document students' participation in the lesson.

Immediately following this observation, the English teachers introduced us to the Japanese practice of conducting post-lesson *hansei kai* (reflection meetings) where we examined evidence and discussed potential lesson revisions. *Hansei* (self-critical reflection) is a fundamental aspect of Japanese culture and routines. For every major event, project, or undertaking, school leaders scheduled a *hansei kai* to thoroughly debrief results and intentionally plan future improvements. Teachers viewed this as an objective exercise and openly embraced feedback on the research lesson.

Lesson Revisions

The *hansei kai* resulted in several changes to our instructional plan and sequence of learning activities. The most significant adjustment was having teachers open with a short model dialogue about their own vacations followed by a similar warm-up exercise where student pairs would spend five minutes freely exchanging questions about summer break (see italicized sections in Table 2.2). We carved out time for this by changing final presentations from all student pairs to a random selection of five pairs.

■ **Table 2.2: Lesson Progression**

Note: Italicized sections reflect changes and additions made to the research lesson between the first and second implementation.

Learning Activities	Expected Student Reactions Teacher Responses and Support	Goals of This Segment Methods of Evaluation
Opening Greeting (1 min.) T: How's it going? S: Great. How's it going? T: Great.	(Part of regular classroom routine)	Typically students begin each lesson by bowing to the teacher and providing a greeting in Japanese. Since this is an English Oral Communication class, we have adopted a routine of having students begin each lesson with a short, informal greeting that they would commonly experience in everyday English conversation.
Introduction to Lesson (4 min.) – *Japanese teacher to explain topic for this lesson: "What did you do this summer?" (written on the board prior to the class).* – *Teachers model a sample conversation for the class about their personal summer vacations. Repeat the conversation twice, so students can practice listening.* – *Ask for volunteers to explain the gist and details in Japanese.*	*Expect students to be listening intently to example conversation and trying to understand what their teachers did over the summer.*	*Goal is to start the lesson by giving students an authentic example of the kind of conversation we are hoping they will learn to produce in the lesson.* *Look for facial expressions, eye contact, levels of attention and engagement.*

(Continued)

■ Table 2.2: (Continued)

Learning Activities	Expected Student Reactions Teacher Responses and Support	Goals of This Segment Methods of Evaluation
Warm-Up Discussion in Pairs (5 min.) – *Have students work in pairs to talk about their summer vacations in English using whatever language they can come up with.* – *Provide students with two simple prompts on the board as conversation starters: "How was your summer vacation?" and "What did you do?"*	*Expect students will have difficulty generating sentences to articulate their experiences and will revert to using a mixture of Japanese and English.* *Teachers circulate to as many pairs as possible simply to listen and see how much English students are able to generate. Avoid interjecting or correcting at this stage. Try to circulate to all students.*	*The purpose of this segment is to engage students in a brief initial attempt to generate conversation without any significant assistance or dialogue structure, both as a diagnostic to see how much language they can produce on their own and to help them measure their own progress from the beginning to the end of the lesson.* *Listen for how much language students are able to produce and what sentence patterns they use to express themselves.*
Introduce Dialogue Exercise (10 min.) – Teachers hand out an example dialogue exercise with a full sequence of exchanges about a student who spent his summer in America and visited Disneyland in California. – Teachers model the conversation for the class one time as they read along. – American teacher reads each line of dialogue and has students repeat phrases to practice pronunciation.	Students will likely struggle with English words that are also incorporated into Japanese *katakana* (such as Disneyland and California). Students will likely struggle with the words *where, anywhere, terrible.* Will also need to practice intonation on: "Not bad," "It was all right," and "It was OK." Students may be unable to translate "It went by too fast."	The focus here is to provide students with an example dialogue structure they can place in their minds so that they can formulate similar sentence patterns on their own in the future. We also want to prepare them for successful practice by modeling correct pronunciation and intonation patterns. *Listen for* areas of difficulty with pronunciation or intonation. Listen for degree to which students speak the lines with meaning versus reading them off in a monotone style without a sense of understanding.

Learning Activities	Expected Student Reactions / Teacher Responses and Support	Goals of This Segment / Methods of Evaluation
– Japanese teacher checks for understanding and calls on students to translate segments of the dialogue into Japanese. – Teachers model the conversation once more.	Teachers will listen for other words that are problematic (not anticipated above) and provide additional practice for students.	
Dialogue Practice in Pairs (10 min.) *(15 min.)* – Students practice in pairs and work to gradually produce the dialogue from memory.	Some students will continue to read the conversation to each other from paper without trying to gradually commit the dialogue to memory. Other students will stop practicing out loud and just work on memorizing the dialogue independently. Also expect some students to just read or speak lines without performing them as dialogue or speaking them with a sense of meaning. Teachers rotate to provide feedback on pronunciation and intonation. Encourage students to gradually work on memorization, and provide additional teaching for students who are repeating the lines as a memorization task without a communicative purpose.	The pair work creates an opportunity not only to memorize the dialogue but to practice speaking the words and phrases multiple times to gain confidence and work on pronunciation. It also gives the teachers an opportunity to listen to students and provide instructive feedback. *Listen for* areas of difficulty with pronunciation or intonation. Listen for degree to which students speak the lines with meaning versus reading them off in a monotone style without a sense of understanding.

(Continued)

■ Table 2.2: (Continued)

Learning Activities	Expected Student Reactions Teacher Responses and Support	Goals of This Segment Methods of Evaluation
	Teachers will discipline amount of time with each pair and try to circulate to all students. *Identify common patterns or areas of difficulty across the class as well as various subgroups (e.g., struggling, intermediate, advanced).*	The pair presentations give teachers the opportunity to point out to the whole class common areas of difficulty with pronunciation and follow up with additional choral repetition. It also provides students with a post-lesson benchmark on their progress compared with their initial attempt at the start of the lesson.
Presentations (30 min.) *(15 min.)* – Have each student pair present the sample dialogue in front of the class (from memory). – *Randomly select five student pairs to perform the dialogue in front of class (from memory).*	Students will struggle with volume, eye contact, and intonation. Some will likely race through the dialogue rather than performing as an actual dialogue and thinking about the words. Teachers provide feedback after each pair and have the whole class work on areas of intonation or pronunciation that were problematic.	*The change to randomly selected pair presentations still provides students with incentive to practice, knowing they might be called on to present in front of class. In addition, using random pairs rather than all students saves more time for modeling and practice during earlier lesson segments.*

Learning Activities	Expected Student Reactions / Teacher Responses and Support	Goals of This Segment / Methods of Evaluation
Final Practice (3–5 min.) – Practice choral repetition once more, pausing to focus on the most problematic sections. – Practice with American teacher as A and then whole class as B. Then switch. Japanese teacher helps lead B. – Japanese teacher provides reminder about grammar assignment that is due tomorrow.	Expect volume and clarity of choral repetition to increase during this final exercise as students speak the words with greater confidence and understanding.	The intent of this final segment is to provide some closure to the class period and give students a sense of accomplishment in their ability to perform the dialogue when compared to the start of the lesson.

The junior high principal also suggested paying closer attention to our use of *kikan shidō* (between-desks instruction), a Japanese term for the guidance and instruction teachers provide while roving between desks to monitor and assist students (Ermeling & Graff-Ermeling, 2014b). He pointed out that teachers focused most of their *kikan shidō* time on a few students who were least comfortable with English, while other students received limited guidance or feedback. He suggested less time with each pair, circulating throughout the room to gain a global perspective of student progress and identifying patterns that warranted whole-class attention. We incorporated these suggestions in the second column of the lesson plan under "Teacher Responses and Support."

Public Research Lesson and Reflection Meeting

For the official public research lesson (*kōkai kenkyū jugyō*) and final *hansei kai,* we modified the 9B class schedule and asked students to assemble after school. We reconstructed the classroom in a large meeting space with extra room on the perimeter for district guests. Observers received a small packet including a general school overview, description of the overall English curriculum, and a copy of the lesson plan to guide observations. Observers remained standing throughout the lesson and moved around quietly on the perimeter during pair work, carefully listening to students' dialogue. They diligently recorded notes on their printed copies of the lesson plan and preserved evidence of what they saw and heard during each learning activity.

The lesson proceeded much as outlined but with an unexpected result during the new opening pair exercise (recently added after the first *hansei kai*). Despite numerous errors in sentence structure and word choice, many students surprised us by producing multiple exchanges about their vacations and sustaining English dialogue for several minutes. This was our first time observing students in spontaneous conversation before they practiced the example dialogue.

Following this warm-up exercise, we proceeded with the other lesson segments, modeling the sample dialogue, leading choral repetition, providing time for practice, and randomly selecting five pairs for final presentations. Each pair performed the dialogue effectively in terms of memorization and delivery. Students struggled with a few proper nouns (e.g., *California, Disneyland*) and reverted to Japanese pronunciation for these words.

Intonation was slightly exaggerated by a few students, and most pairs still struggled with the phrase, "It was all right." One student pair had a less convincing delivery, repeating lines rapidly without a sense of communicative purpose. We finished with additional practice and choral repetition focused on these areas of difficulty.

After dismissing students for the day, we reconfigured the room for a formal *hansei kai*. Observers sat in student desks, and the two presenting teachers sat in front, facing the participants. A district leader sat next to the presenting teachers and moderated discussion using the same structured protocol we had observed in previous lesson study events. He thanked us for hosting the research lesson and asked the presenting teachers to initiate the *hansei kai* with comments and reflections on the lesson. Brad made a brief statement complimenting students' efforts to master the sample dialogue and noted several challenges with pronunciation requiring further attention in future class periods. The other presenting teacher expressed partial satisfaction with student engagement and conversation but highlighted her ongoing struggle with several students who refused to use English during activities and reverted to Japanese during dialogue exercises. She cited specific examples from the research lesson and solicited advice for engaging reluctant speakers. Prompted by the moderator, she also explained the connection between the lesson design and our school-wide emphasis on independence and self-reliance.

The moderator then invited observers to report on their lesson observations and findings related to the research theme "fostering students' initiative in communication," and the specific lesson goal "sustaining dialogue about recent past vacation activities." One participant shared several observations from the opening warm-up exercise where students used a wide range of vocabulary and sentence patterns: "I noticed at least two pairs were exchanging questions such as, 'Did you get a jet lag? Did you gain weight? Did you shopping? Was it expensive?' This suggests to me," she continued, "that perhaps the students were already capable of initiating more conversation than the lesson anticipated, since the example dialogue structure provided later in the lesson was more simplistic than the sentence patterns students independently created."

Building on this observation, a second participant described another student pair that tailored the sample dialogue to make it more relevant and personal. "They adjusted the dialogue," he explained, "while keeping an eye on the teacher as if in fear of breaking rules of the activity. For example, one student added a question about favorite rides at Disneyland, and the other student changed his response about American food, saying, 'I love to eat hamburgers.' "

The observer suggested, "These responses provide evidence that the exercise had effectively captured students' interest, but they also suggest memorizing the example dialogue may have constrained students from applying sentence patterns in a more authentic way. Perhaps," he proposed, "it would be productive to have students revise the dialogue, make it more personal, and then receive feedback on necessary corrections as they practice."

Another participant noted similar observations. She suggested an alternative closing activity where students would again practice talking about their own summer vacations, as they did in the opening warm-up, but this time using the new sentence patterns acquired during the lesson.

The moderator paused the group several times to synthesize observations or comments and discuss implications related to the design rationale. He also probed for insights and applications for other courses and grade levels.

Final Reflections
From the English Team

Over the next several weeks, we joined our English department colleagues for two additional meetings to revisit observations and findings from the *hansei kai* and compile final project reflections. The evidence collected over the course of both implementations exposed important shortcomings in our lesson design and distinctly altered some of the department's basic assumptions about teaching oral communication.

First, we had dramatically underestimated students' abilities to engage in spontaneous conversation about immediate past events. Although we selected conversation topics of high interest to students, we overstructured the dialogue practice in ways that constrained them from engaging in authentic and personally relevant exchanges. We especially noted observers' suggestions for allowing students to revise the dialogue and receive feedback as they practiced. We also appreciated the idea of closing the lesson with a final pair exercise, repeating the opening conversation about students' own summer vacations. This would encourage immediate application of the new dialogue structure and provide a pre- and post-benchmark of student progress during the lesson.

Second, we discussed observational feedback that highlighted a disproportionate emphasis on the lowest-performing students. The examples recorded of student pairs secretly improvising with the script clearly revealed how our lesson design had limited students' opportunities for more advanced dialogue and spontaneous conversation. The department agreed to continue collaborating around lesson ideas and activities that would appropriately challenge and meet the needs of intermediate and advanced students without neglecting the lower-performing subgroup. Based on the principal's insight from our first research lesson, we also agreed to monitor our between-desks instruction (*kikan shidō*) to more equally distribute time and attention throughout the class, identify patterns of student progress or areas of need, and make appropriate mid-lesson adjustments.

Last, teachers discussed the importance of intentionally and regularly evaluating alignment between lesson design and stated learning goals. The written goal for this lesson was to foster students' initiative in communicating and sustaining dialogue about immediate past vacation experiences, but we operated with a separate, unstated goal of having students perform a well-rehearsed example dialogue with accurate pronunciation and intonation. This distracted us from the lesson purpose and restricted opportunities for student initiative with English.

This final lesson study gathering ended around 7:30 p.m., placing us among the last group of teachers preparing to leave the *shokuin shitsu* after a long day of teaching. As a daily routine beginning around 5:30 p.m., teachers would gradually take turns making a humble exit. Before leaving, each teacher would perform a slight bow and quietly say, "*Osaki ni shitsurei shimasu.*" (I am deeply sorry for being so rude as to leave before you.) Any remaining faculty still working at their desks would typically respond with, "*Otsukaresama deshita.*" (You must be very tired. Thank you for your hard work.) As we completed these long hours of multiple reflection sessions, we recall exiting the room that evening, bowing deeply and expressing the standard apology for our "early exit" as a dozen or so teachers (mostly from the English department) remained working. The choral reply, "*Otsukaresama deshita,*" carried a whole new meaning, complete with memories of all we had accomplished and learned together through the lesson study experience.

Insights Gained From Our Apprenticeship: Essential Skills and Mindsets

The preceding account provides a unique perspective of American teachers living in Japan and immersed in authentic Japanese lesson study. In this section we summarize the skills we needed to develop and the shifts in mindset we experienced while learning to participate alongside Japanese colleagues as active members in the lesson study process.

Fashioning a Coherent Lesson Storyline

Throughout the lesson study process, Japanese teachers challenged us to shift our thinking and grow our capacity in fashioning a coherent, well-scripted lesson storyline—the overall sequence or progression of lesson activities that helps students advance toward identified learning goals. Teachers began the planning phase by building consensus around the main elements of the storyline and relied on this as a unifying framework to guide planning, implementation, and observations. The storyline evolved from group discussion around a series of key questions like the following:

> What do we want students to understand or be able to do at the end of this lesson or series of lessons? What evidence will we collect during and after the lesson to help us evaluate student progress and study the relationship between teaching and learning?

> What prior knowledge and background experience will students bring to this lesson? What will most students already know, or what assumptions will they have? What common misconceptions might we expect? What related content or prerequisite knowledge will be covered prior to the lesson?

> What combination and order of learning activities will help students progress toward these learning goals? How will each individual activity connect and build on the previous activity? How will it pave the way for subsequent learning activities? What are the specific teacher and student roles for each individual activity that will best facilitate the desired outcome?

As American-trained teachers working to participate in this process, we had no prior experience systematically addressing these questions or fashioning a storyline to guide the construction of a detailed research lesson. Our experience largely focused on fragmented planning of individual lesson elements, managing efficient distribution of time, and incorporating a variety of learning activities or delivery methods. We paid limited attention to the coherence and flow of the larger narrative structure and how the sequence of activities combined to support lesson goals.

In addition to creating coherence during the planning process, our experience highlights the value of the storyline during lesson implementation where it serves as an operational guide to clarify teacher and student roles. The use of *kikan shidō* provides a helpful illustration. Before this lesson study project, Brad typically approached all pair work sessions with a singular mindset of circulating to students who needed the most attention. The junior high principal helped us recognize that the teacher's role during student pair work—what we chose to focus on, how long we spent with each pair, and what we chose to say or not say—had a specific instructional value related to the overall lesson storyline. We recorded these *kikan shidō* reminders in the "Teacher Responses and Support" column of the lesson plan and thoroughly reviewed these notes prior to the second implementation. In this way, the storyline functioned much like a teacher global positioning system (GPS) during the lesson—a reminder of not only the lesson sequence but also the essential teacher actions for each learning activity.

The storyline played an equally important role during reflection and revision. In the account reported here, in addition to the notes about *kikan shidō,* the group added two opening exercises to the beginning of the storyline and altered the structure of the final segment to make time for these additions. The storyline provided the group with an accessible, shared framework for productively identifying and discussing these key lesson segments and modifications.

Articulating and Testing Working Hypotheses

Another area of emphasis we observed with Japanese colleagues was the continual effort to articulate rationale for each element of the instructional design. As we composed the "Plan to Guide Teaching and Learning" (see Table 2.1), the Japanese teachers crafted a working hypothesis for how this sequence of activities addressed the lesson, unit, and overall project goals. They did the same for each individual lesson segment, explaining goals and rationales for the learning activity in the far right column of the lesson progression. During the post-lesson *hansei kai,* the moderator facilitated analysis of these ideas and suppositions based on evidence collected from observations. Even when lesson results revealed gaps in reasoning behind the design, as was the case with the project reported here, having a recorded hypothesis or rationale made it possible to reflect meaningfully on the lesson and make revisions based on our latest findings.

This repeated emphasis on justifying and explaining lesson choices was unlike anything we had experienced with lesson planning in the United States.

We were accustomed to writing lesson objectives and identifying learning activities. We generally understood the importance of selecting activities aligned with intended outcomes, but there was no cognitive process in place for deliberately articulating and monitoring these choices.

Learning to incorporate this additional element as part of the lesson study process helped us think more carefully about cause-effect relationships between instructional choices and student learning—to better understand and predict how teaching influences learning and how student responses, in turn, influence teaching moves. For example, when students surprised us with their ability to produce spontaneous English conversation, it compelled us to rethink our working hypothesis and reconsider assumptions about how students learn to communicate. It prompted us to question existing instructional practices (e.g., asking students to memorize example dialogues) and increased our curiosity in alternative approaches. We discovered the purpose of conducting a carefully planned research lesson was not to produce an exemplary lesson or evaluate individual teachers, as was our typical experience with classroom observations in the United States. Instead, the purpose was to create a laboratory for collective inquiry. The presenting teacher was simply a vehicle for testing out these carefully crafted hypotheses so that a community of teachers could observe and study the effect on student learning.

Relying on Evidence to Guide Planning and Reflection

A third critical skill required for lesson study was the effective use of evidence to guide planning and reflection. The Japanese teachers relied on evidence to support their work at each stage of the process, beginning with the use of student work, observation records, and survey data to guide selection of a research theme. During instructional planning, teachers documented key indicators of progress and methods of evaluation for each successive learning activity. These notes were preserved in the far right column of the lesson plan as a tool to guide observers during lesson implementation. The design of the post-lesson *hansei kai* also facilitated careful examination of observational data and student work products. Each comment observers contributed included specific descriptions of evidence to support their statements or conjectures. The moderator summarized these comments and probed for more details, asking for similar or disparate examples to continue the discussion. As the group transitioned from the reflective discussion to the revision process, they continued to rely on these evidence-based findings to guide lesson adjustments and future plans.

While our background and training in the United States included some emphasis on assessment and references to evidence-based decision making, we had no prior experience focusing on evidence with this level of depth and rigor. We previously associated evidence with quizzes, tests, homework, and grades but were not accustomed to analyzing classroom interactions and artifacts as potential sources of evidence. When planning lessons, we primarily focused on identifying information, activities, and exercises for each segment of the class period but did not systematically consider points of evaluation for each instructional interval. When observing lessons, we focused more on teacher behaviors or superficial aspects of the classroom environment. When asked to reflect and make revisions, our first instinct was to comment on whether the lesson went as planned and whether students were generally engaged.

Through the example of our colleagues, we eventually developed a new set of cognitive disciplines for collecting student data during observations and supporting post-lesson comments with clear references to evidence. This was modeled for us by lesson observers who focused observations on small groups of students and carefully recorded notes for use during the *hansei kai* (e.g., utterances of students' spontaneous conversation about jet lag and shopping, or carefully preserved observations of students secretly altering the example dialogue). These experiences broadened our understanding of classroom evidence and heightened our awareness of the data sources available for monitoring student progress and guiding instructional decisions. They also helped us recognize that if the goal was to improve teaching as measured by evidence, then insights gained from instructional miscues could be just as valuable as insights gained from instructional successes.

Embracing Collaboration and Collective Ownership of Improvement

As illustrated with the teachers' room diagram (Figure 2.2), our lesson study work was situated within a cultural context defined by collaboration and reciprocal accountability. For our Japanese colleagues, collaboration was a way of life, not a strategy adopted for selected meetings or projects. Teachers met informally throughout the day to plan lessons, discuss ideas, and visit each other's classrooms.

This spirit of collaboration and collective ownership was even more pronounced during lesson study. Teachers relied on each other to shape and guide development of detailed lesson plans. Regardless of age, experience, or who was presenting the lesson, teachers referred to the instructional plan as a collective responsibility and jointly owned set of ideas. During lesson observations, they worked as a team to distribute themselves around the room and capture evidence from multiple student perspectives. When observers offered suggestions or constructive criticism, such as the junior high principal's suggestion about improving use of *kikan shidō,* the entire group took ownership of the suggestion as a useful idea for improving *our* lesson.

While the idea of professional learning communities is now commonplace in most U.S. schools, the terms *learning community* and *teacher collaboration* are loosely defined and rarely used to reference the kind of commitment to joint improvement exemplified in Japanese settings (Ermeling & Gallimore, 2013). We had previously viewed teaching as mostly a private activity with maximum autonomy and limited interaction with colleagues. We were not accustomed to such a transparent environment where teaching and learning problems (e.g., fostering initiative with communication) became shared problems, and successes were jointly celebrated. This was both exciting and challenging as it required a significant amount of trust and willingness to sacrifice our own personal preferences for the sake of a collective effort. It also required that we remain objective and remember comments and suggestions, such as "improving our *kikan shidō* practices" or "giving students more opportunity for spontaneous dialogue," were intended as feedback on the team's lesson design, not a critique of the presenting teacher.

We improved over time in adopting this collective mindset and learned to view the lesson as a joint product. We also learned to appreciate the power of conducting observations as a team, affording us a shared reference point and opportunity to see our instructional ideas in action rather than merely share or debate "best practices." Most importantly, as illustrated in our final exit from the teachers' room as the project concluded, we began to recognize our shared responsibility for teaching and learning and to view ourselves as part of a culture and community that was perpetually working together toward a common set of goals.

Persisting With Problems Over Time

A final insight gained from our lesson study apprenticeship was learning to persist with problems over time and embrace the slow, steady process of instructional improvement. The Japanese teachers spent multiple years investigating a single research theme and worked persistently to revise and improve each research lesson through several iterations of planning and reflection. They worked for long hours, celebrated small improvements, and measured progress by what they learned, not by how quickly they achieved results. We observed this same mindset during each school visitation for other district lesson study events. The widespread acceptance of this steady, relentless process is one primary way Japanese educators have worked to improve teaching practice over many decades (Chichibu & Kihara, 2013; Sarkar Arani, Keisuke, & Lassegard, 2010).

By contrast, most newly certified U.S. teachers enter a culture that demands immediate results and offers little tolerance for incremental improvement. The training activities we experienced in the United States were typically brief, episodic workshops and generic training sessions during faculty meetings. These events shaped our expectations of professional learning as a largely passive endeavor requiring minimal time, effort, or follow-through.

Our lesson study experience challenged us to transcend these pervasive norms and remain hungry, remain humble, and remain curious. It taught us to be patient with our own learning as well as others' and required that we embrace questions and obstacles in our practice as opportunities to grow and improve. This was not an easy adjustment. Spending many hours over a period of months to plan and study a single lesson initially seemed excessively tedious and disproportionate to the large volume of lessons in our curriculum. It was difficult to remain patient during multiple iterations of lesson revision and willingly subject a well-thought-out plan and rationale to further scrutiny and refinement. But the end result, like the rich drop of food coloring, was a deep, pervasive knowledge that profoundly shaped our practice and had a lasting effect on decisions about teaching and learning.

Conclusion

Like other researchers who have reported benefits of lesson study, we believe it has potential to profoundly change the way U.S. educators approach improvement of teaching and learning.

Essential Skills and Mindsets for Lesson Study

1. Fashioning a coherent storyline
2. Articulating and testing a working hypothesis
3. Relying on evidence to guide planning and reflection
4. Embracing collaboration and collective ownership of improvement
5. Persisting with problems over time

Our experience provides additional evidence that American teachers can learn to participate in lesson study and embrace incremental improvement. Our experience also suggests that the skills and mind-sets required to participate effectively may not be instinctive or easily acquired. Other U.S. teachers learning to conduct lesson study will need significant time and resources to gain understanding and appreciation for what it means to fashion a coherent storyline, articulate and test hypotheses, rely on evidence to guide reflection, embrace collective ownership of improvement, and persist with problems over time.

The success of lesson study outside of Japan will continue to depend on the level of commitment practitioners have to understanding these skills and mindsets, the rationale behind the way lesson study is designed, and the conditions that support authentic lesson study. Just as the lesson study process requires a persistent commitment over time to improve teaching and learning, leaders and practitioners will benefit from adopting a similar mindset of patience with the slow, steady process of effective implementation: taking time to develop a solid foundation of lesson study principles, carefully and incrementally testing out adaptations to evaluate their effectiveness, and diligently working toward deep, substantive change and lasting results.

The next chapter describes our effort to facilitate a similar lesson study process while conducting research with a group of high school teachers in the United States. We chronicle the insights they gained from planning and observing lessons with colleagues and embracing new approaches to shared problems of practice. We also provide analysis and suggestions for designing effective U.S. implementation.

REFLECTION QUESTIONS

KEY PRINCIPLE: *Steady, concentrated effort over time produces a rich, permeating, and lasting effect.*

1. What aspects of this lesson study account were insightful for you? What aspects of this story did you find challenging to imagine in a U.S. context?

2. How does the collaborative process described in this chapter differ from the work you are doing in your collaborative settings? How is it similar?

3. Take a few minutes to reflect on each of the essential skills and mindsets described at the end of this chapter. Which of these represents an underdeveloped skill or mindset for teachers in your school context? Which of these might be an underdeveloped skill for you personally?

4. What are the benefits of focusing on deep planning and analysis of individual lessons? What adjustments might be required to embrace this kind of approach?

ADDITIONAL RESOURCES

- See Leader's Guide in the Appendix for additional team exercises from this chapter and presentation ideas for the "Rich Drop of Food Coloring" portrait.
- Visit the companion website to download presentation slides, including a full color digital image of the portrait. Also find customizable templates, checklists, and tools to assist your implementation efforts.

Available at http://www.corwin.com/ErmelingTeachingBetter

REFERENCES

Carroll, T., Fulton, K., & Doerr, H. (2010). *Team up for 21st century teaching and learning: What research and practice reveal about professional learning.* Washington, DC: National Commission on Teaching and America's Future.

Chichibu, T., & Kihara, T. (2013). How Japanese schools build a professional learning community by lesson study. *International Journal for Lesson and Learning Studies, 2*(1), 12–25.

Ermeling, B. A., & Gallimore, R. (2013). Learning to be a community: Schools need adaptable models to create successful programs. *Journal of Staff Development (JSD), 34*(2), 42–45.

Ermeling, B. A., & Graff-Ermeling, G. (2014a). Learning to learn from teaching: A first-hand account of lesson study in Japan. *International Journal for Lesson and Learning Studies, 3*(2), 170–192.

Ermeling, B. A., & Graff-Ermeling, G. (2014b). Teaching between desks. *Educational Leadership, 72*(2), 55–60.

Fernandez, C., Cannon, J., & Chokshi, S. M. (2003). A US–Japan lesson study collaboration reveals critical lenses for examining practice. *Teaching and Teacher Education, 19*(2), 171–185.

Lewis, C. (2002). *Lesson study: A handbook of teacher-led instructional change.* Philadelphia, PA: Research for Better Schools.

Lewis, C., Perry, R., & Murata, A. (2006). How should research contribute to instructional improvement? The case of lesson study. *Educational Researcher, 35*(3), 3–14.

Lewis, C., & Takahashi, A. (2013). Facilitating curriculum reforms through lesson study. *International Journal for Lesson and Learning Studies, 2*(3), 207–217.

Sarkar Arani, M., Keisuke, F., & Lassegard, J. (2010). Lesson study as professional culture in Japanese schools. *Japan Review, 22*, 171–200.

Stigler, J., & Hiebert, J. (1999). *The teaching gap: Best ideas from the world's teachers for improving education in the classroom.* New York, NY: Free Press.

This chapter was adapted from previously published work in the following:

Ermeling, B. A., & Graff-Ermeling, G. (2014). Learning to learn from teaching: A first-hand account of lesson study in Japan. *International Journal for Lesson and Learning Studies, 3*(2), 170–192. ©2014 Brad and Genevieve Ermeling. Selected by Emerald Publishing and the World Association of Lesson Studies as the 2015 "Outstanding Paper of the Year."

CHAPTER 3

Expanding Horizons

A Case Study of U.S. Teachers Collaborating to Change Practice

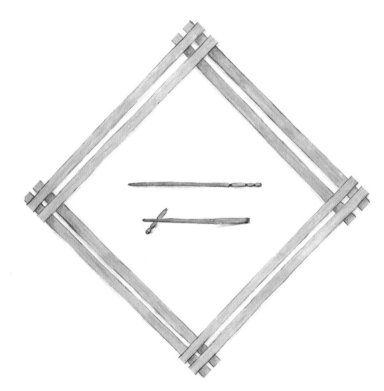

Japanese Toothpick (Tsumayōji)

PORTRAIT #3: Japanese Toothpick (*Tsumayōji*)

As cultural practices are imitated and repeated over time, they become ingrained and difficult to change. They also place significant limits on our *horizons of observation*—the boundaries of what tools, interactions, and behaviors we have been exposed to and imagine as possible within a given social context (Hutchins, 1993, p. 52). We imitate what we have seen and grow accustomed to what we know and have always known. Sometimes the best way to expand our horizon of observation with a particular practice is to place ourselves in a completely new context and observe another approach that jolts our thinking, causing us to view our own culture and practices from a fresh perspective.

Consider the cultural practice for using a toothpick as an illustration of this point. An individual who has little or no experience outside of Western culture will pay almost no attention to the design of a typical Western-style toothpick. It's a practical tool people use to clean their teeth. Both ends of the toothpick are sharpened, so it can be used multiple times with either side. It's cheap, simple, and disposable—nothing special about it. It's likely that most people in Western culture have never considered the possibility of a toothpick designed another way.

Now consider the design and cultural practice for using a Japanese toothpick (*tsumayōji*). At a first glance, one might notice a few obvious similarities. It's sharp on one end and has a similar length and width, but it also has some distinct differences that can be quickly overlooked and underappreciated. When using the *tsumayōji,* a Japanese person always covers his or her mouth with one hand while using the other hand to maneuver the toothpick for cleaning. This is considered proper etiquette and prevents the individual from accidentally flicking any loose food particles on dining companions. It also stems from an ancient Buddhist belief that showing any bone in public (including teeth) is dirty and inappropriate.

Following the same careful attention to cleanliness, after using the toothpick, Japanese are careful not to place the used tip of the *tsumayōji* directly on a dirty table or plate. Instead, the *tsumayōji* itself is designed with a built-in mechanism that becomes a holder for the business end of the toothpick. There are two narrow ridges carved into the decorative end of the *tsumayōji*. The lowest ridge (see image at the beginning of the chapter) can be folded and snapped off, so the toothpick is now separated into two parts. The small part with the remaining decorative ridge is set on the table, and the business end fits snugly in the ridge as a holder for the *tsumayōji,* much like a chopstick holder. This protects the toothpick from contamination with the table, so it can be used again later in the meal as needed. It also signals to others that the toothpick has already been used, so they don't accidentally pick it up, assuming it's clean.

The *tsumayōji* illustrates several values in Japanese culture such as attention to detail, cleanliness, proper etiquette, careful craftsmanship, and elegant presentation. A comparison with the Western-style toothpick also reveals several values of Western culture, such as practicality, functionality, simplicity, and the value of economy and efficiency over elegance or presentation.

Both toothpicks clean teeth, but coming from a Western perspective, being exposed to the *tsumayōji* offers a completely different view and expands the boundaries of possibilities for how a toothpick might be designed and used. It also serves as a catalyst for reflection on the values and traditions that underlie one's practice and routines, which otherwise would remain unnoticed and unexamined.

The same is true with teaching practices. Teaching is a cultural activity that has been imitated and learned over time from at least 16 years of observation that all educators experience growing up as students in classrooms. As a result, teachers are accustomed to certain methods or *cultural scripts* for teaching math or science, or any subject, and can't easily see beyond that horizon to imagine other possibilities (Gallimore, 1996).

Exploring a variety of examples from other countries and school communities is one way to broaden horizons and gain exposure to alternative practices— both for teaching and for the process of improving teaching. As illustrated with the story in this chapter, sometimes even observing and studying examples of teaching with colleagues in the same school or district, who have set aside traditional scripts to investigate and learn alternative approaches, can help catalyze deep and meaningful reflection and create the circumstances for change.

Lesson Study Comes to a U.S. High School

As another school year kicked off, Amy was beginning her 28th year of teaching. Her current assignment was high school biology. Ken was entering his 9th year as a teacher of chemistry, Tom his 35th year in that same subject area, and Jim was beginning year 14 of teaching high school physics (teacher names are pseudonyms). All were committed teachers, respected by their colleagues, passionate about their subject matter, and eager to help students explore the world of science. They worked at a large, comprehensive high school about 40 miles outside of Los Angeles, California.

The school year began much like years past. Faculty met for a series of introductory meetings and listened to the standard parade of announcements from administrators regarding new attendance policies, dress code, parking instructions for staff, and changes in the bell schedule. Amy, Ken, Tom, and Jim also attended science department meetings to discuss items that still needed to be ordered—new laptops for the physics lab upstairs, a new scale for the biology teachers, and so on. They briefly discussed a new lab report format and shared a few ideas for incorporating Internet searches into their regular lab activities. Teachers then spent the balance of their time working individually in their classrooms to prepare for the school year.

This year, Amy, Ken, Tom, and Jim also volunteered for something a bit different. We asked them to consider participating in a research project to test out a version of the lesson study process we experienced in Japan and investigate its potential impact in an American high school context. Accepting our invitation, they agreed to become a team of science teachers that would meet regularly across the year and work through two cycles of planning, implementation, and reflection on research lessons. The specific process we outlined for them involved the following iterative phases (also represented in Figure 3.1).

- Identify a research theme (recursive teaching and learning problem).
- Identify a context for study (specific unit and lesson topic in the curriculum).
- Study the curriculum and related research to develop a working hypothesis.

- Develop a plan to guide teaching and learning, including a detailed research lesson.
- Implement the research lesson, and collect evidence from observations and student work.
- Examine evidence, and study the relationship between teaching and learning.
- Revise and repeat the process to continue studying the problem.
- Reflect and record insights about teaching and learning.

Brad played the role of facilitator for the group, and Genevieve assisted with data collection and project planning. The teachers made all decisions related to the content of the process, including the problem they would address and the instructional solutions they would plan and implement.

■ Figure 3.1: Lesson Study Cycle

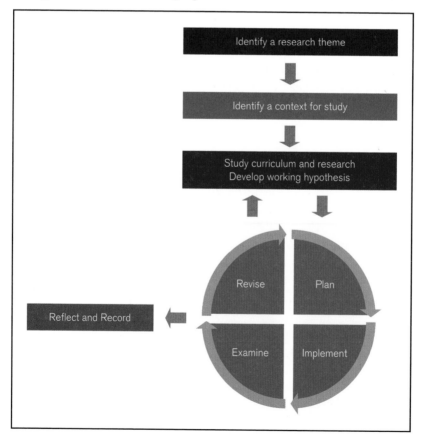

Video-Based Lesson Observations

As part of the project design and research, we substituted the use of video for live observations using a web-based video platform called "Visibility" from the LessonLab Research Institute.[1] Teachers accessed the platform to conduct asynchronous review and analysis as well as collect and record observational evidence from the lessons. For each lesson study cycle, we chose one classroom context as the primary "laboratory" for planning and video analysis (see Table 3.1), but we also collectively developed instructional plans and recorded lesson videos for each of the four subject areas. These lessons were available for additional reflection and analysis after teachers completed viewing the primary research lesson.

Brad encoded the videos, uploaded them to the platform, and prepared the videos for analysis, including time code links for each main segment of instruction. Along with each time code link, Brad also restated the purpose for the lesson segment (as noted in the jointly developed instructional plan) and directed teachers to record observations of student learning related to that segment. During each iteration of the process, teachers completed their review of the selected research lesson after the implementation of their own lesson and prior to the face-to-face debrief session. We then used the video comments and analysis to ground our reflective discussion in evidentiary observations.

Project Phases and Time

The team spent approximately 22 hours working through the inquiry process. Sixty percent of this time took place in the traditional setting of face-to-face meetings, and 40 percent took place online, using the Visibility platform. Figure 3.2 provides an overview of the project phases and length of time devoted to each phase. The team also spent an additional six to seven hours in project introductions, preparation and logistics, practice with the technology platform, and preparing project reports.

Identifying a Research Theme

At the outset of the project, Brad facilitated a review of recent writing samples from student lab reports in each subject area to help the team identify

---

[1] Visibility is no longer an active software application. Zaption (at http://www.zaption.com) is a comparable application with enhanced features for studying, commenting, and collaborating around lesson videos.

■ **Figure 3.2: Lesson Study Project Phases and Time Estimates**

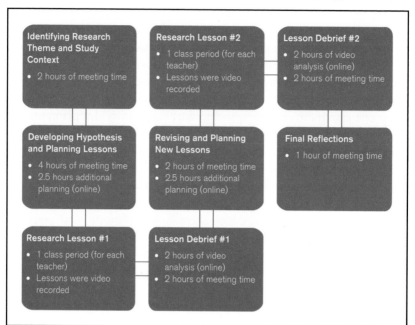

a shared instructional challenge. This analysis revealed a common concern: students were not grappling with the underlying concepts related to velocity and acceleration, the role of structure and function in living organisms, or balancing chemical equations. Instead, students were mostly "regurgitating facts" and "following lab procedures like recipes from a cookbook." Despite rigorous standards and a rigorous science curriculum teachers had used for years, students continued to struggle with reasoning and applying scientific knowledge to solve novel problems.

Drawing from these writing samples, the group worked to develop a draft description of the research theme and targeted learning outcome. What follows is the initial phrasing that emerged from the group's discussion and several key terms the group identified to ensure mutual understanding.

Research Theme (teaching and learning problem):

Reasoning and applying scientific knowledge

Targeted Learning Outcome (if problem is successfully addressed):

Students will be able think beyond the basic facts to discover and articulate concepts about natural phenomena through *multi-semiotic* modes and apply and *transfer* those concepts in different settings.

Important Definitions:

> *Multi-semiotic* = Verbal, mathematical, and/or graphical modes of scientific communication (Wellington & Osborne, 2001).

> *Near transfer* = An individual's ability to apply previously learned scientific knowledge, skills, and methods to manipulate, analyze, synthesize, create and/or evaluate a new situation that is "closely similar but not identical" (Haskell, 2001, p. 29). An example of near transfer is explaining why a company that manufactures chemical products would need to make use of balanced equations.

The group also identified several key lesson contexts in each of their subjects that might serve as meaningful opportunities for studying this problem across two iterations of inquiry. Table 3.1 provides a list of the lesson contexts they selected. The primary research lesson for each cycle is distinguished with a bold font.

■ Table 3.1: Lesson Contexts

Subject Area and Teacher	Lesson Contexts for Studying "Reasoning and Applying Scientific Knowledge" (across two lesson study cycles)	
AP Chemistry *(Tom)*	Lesson 1: Redox	Lesson 2: Calorimetry
AP Biology *(Amy)*	Lesson 1: Dissolved Oxygen in Water	**Lesson 2: Osmosis and Diffusion**
Physics *(Jim)*	**Lesson 1: Graphical Methods**	Lesson 2: Acceleration
Honors Chemistry *(Ken)*	Lesson 1: Principles of Measurement	Lesson 2: Atomic Structure

Developing a Working Hypothesis

Having identified a research theme and initial study context, the group spent the next several meetings reviewing curriculum and discussing types of evidence and criteria that could be used to measure student progress with *transfer of knowledge.* They also studied research summaries we provided from Bransford, Brown, and Cocking (2000) and Haskell (2001) and began crafting a working hypothesis for the upcoming research lesson. Bransford et al. emphasized the importance of *making students' thinking visible,* and Haskell provided a theory called *deep-context teaching,* describing how students' erroneous conceptions block understanding of scientific phenomena.

Shift From "Telling" to Productive Struggle

As the conversation evolved, the team noted a strong parallel between the problem of misconceptions they observed in the student work analyzed during the previous meeting and the need for exposing and addressing misconceptions, as described in the transfer research. This wouldn't change, the teachers agreed, until they stopped relying on lectures and lab procedures that emphasized telling and memorizing. Teaching needed to focus on building deeper understanding, and students needed more opportunities to engage in and persist with challenging tasks.

Lesson Storyline: Struggle/Scaffold Script

They agreed to begin jointly planning lessons to hone their skills with inquiry teaching. The first iteration of lessons would feature a *card sort activity*—an instructional strategy described in the transfer literature for promoting student struggle and surfacing misconceptions. Using these ideas as a guide, the team drafted a basic storyline of lesson steps, which they later titled the *struggle/scaffold script.*

1. Implement a productive struggle activity (e.g., card sort strategy) to engage students with scientific concepts and surface students' conceptions and misconceptions.

2. Withhold reference materials before and during the struggle stage.

3. Suspend verbal guidance and "telling" during the struggle stage.

4. Create opportunities to see students' thinking and reasoning (e.g., concept map, presentation, written explanation or rationale).

5. Note misconceptions for future reference; preserve student work and conceptual organization for follow-up lessons or assignments.

6. Tailor instruction, assignments, and activities to build on students' ideas, address misconceptions, and scaffold student learning.

7. Provide opportunities for students to privately or publicly resolve misconceptions and articulate new understandings.

8. Design assessment activities or writing assignments that include a *transfer of learning* prompt.

Of the four group members, Jim had spent the most time experimenting with productive struggle in his previous teaching practice. Throughout the planning discussions, Jim provided numerous insights, ideas, and suggestions that shaped the team's understanding of the subtle pedagogical choices behind implementing this well. The following exchange between Jim and Amy is one important example:

Jim: One thing that I found that might be problematic is that students don't let go of misconceptions very easily. And I've seen the situation several times where you have them expose the misconceptions, but they're not really exposing them to themselves; they're just exposing them to you.

Amy: That is profound.

Jim: You go ahead and teach the lesson.

Amy: Um hmm.

Jim: And you think, "OK, well they're going to pick up on all these things . . ." and then you give a test, and they give you exactly what they did originally. . . . It takes a little bit of student work. When the students discover they have a misconception, then they're more ready to change that.

Each of the other three members openly acknowledged that this was a rather unfamiliar approach but something they were eager to embrace and attempt.

Round 1: Uneven Attempts

In our next sequence of meetings, the group jointly developed detailed research lessons for each of their subject areas that incorporated these struggle/scaffold components. Jim's lesson (primary study context for Cycle 1) focused on graphing motion, Amy's lesson focused on dissolved oxygen in water, Ken's lesson focused on measurement, and Tom's lesson focused on oxidation reduction reactions (redox).

Despite deliberate and extensive planning efforts, there was significant variation in the results for the first round of lesson implementation. We summarize two examples below: the physics research lesson (implemented by Jim) and the AP biology lesson (implemented by Amy).

Physics Research Lesson: Struggle Is a Comfort Zone

The physics research lesson involved a challenging *struggle activity* that surfaced a number of student misconceptions about graphing motion. The lesson plan the team developed placed students into six groups with each team assigned a unique, real-life scenario involving motion. Jim asked the students to sort through a set of index cards featuring various graphing labels and determine how to graph the motion described in the scenario. The students were required to complete their graphs on small whiteboards and explain their scenarios to the class. Below is an example of one scenario students were asked to consider.

A Fast Break With the Football

You are walking along in the park one day, and you suddenly realize that the sack lunch you were holding is actually an oversized plastic football. You panic and begin running furiously toward two closely spaced power poles that you have mistaken as the uprights of a goalpost. You run 65 yards in 25 seconds to make the touchdown. Overjoyed with your fantastic moves, you spike the ball heartily, only to find out that your thermos has broken.

As anticipated during planning discussions, many students mistakenly attributed "speeding up" to an upward-sloping line and "slowing down" to a downward-sloping line, which only works for objects with a positive velocity. Many students also mistakenly viewed a sloped line as an actual picture of an object's movement—say, something moving in a northwesterly direction—rather than recognizing the slope as a representation of displacement over time.

One reason misconceptions like this persist is that students' primary exposure to graphing in math class typically involves repetitive practice with abstract formulas and equations, with minimal application to real-life scenarios. By challenging students to create their own graphs for the types of motion they encounter in everyday life—a football flying through the air, a car screeching to a halt, or a body moving back and forth while dancing—the lesson helped students begin to make a conceptual connection between the image of the graph and the data it represents.

Throughout the card sort activity, Jim consistently suspended guidance and encouraged struggle as the students voiced their confusion with the task and looked to Jim for answers and assistance. When a student asked, "Are those supposed to be something?," Jim calmly responded with, "They all have something to do with something." And when another student exclaimed, "I have never been this confused in my life," Jim answered with a smile, "That's a comfort zone, a place to grow from." No textbooks or other materials were made available during the period, and students were not told about the activity in advance. While the level of dissonance was high, the struggle was not so difficult that students completely gave up or ran out of time to complete the task. Some groups needed more encouragement than others, but all groups completed the activity and came up with a graphical explanation for their scenario. Jim then looked for opportunities to uncover students' misconceptions and solidify their understanding, providing timely explanations such as, "We're not just using x and y. We have real things that go on these axes, real things that change and that we're going to be measuring." Jim also followed up the lesson with a transfer prompt assignment, which required students to apply this graphing knowledge with a series of mathematical expressions.

AP Biology Lesson: Shielding Students From Struggle

Things went differently for some of the other teachers. Amy's story was especially interesting. For the AP biology class, the group designed a lab activity to help students understand how complex variables influence the dissolved oxygen content of water and affect biological activity in aquatic environments. The students were to sort through pictures of different bodies of water and place the pictures on a grid, using prior knowledge and reasoning to order the pictures by estimated water temperature (horizontal axis) and levels of oxygen content (vertical axis). Specifically, students would need to estimate how environmental factors such as climate, salinity, water movement, and the surrounding ecosystem might influence levels of oxygen content.

During the group planning session for this lesson, Amy wrote down in her notes and expressed to the group that she would not provide students with a copy of the lab worksheet in advance that included a detailed explanation of main concepts and variables that influence levels of oxygen. Nevertheless, a few days before the lesson, Amy began feeling anxious about the confusion this might cause her students as well as the amount of class time the activity would require. Compelled by these concerns, she altered the plan and decided to distribute the lab worksheet for homework during the preceding class period. She reasoned that students were not accustomed to this kind of anxiety or confusion in the classroom and needed a certain amount of information to complete the activity successfully and efficiently.

During the sorting task, rather than persist with the challenge of thinking through complex variables, most students went directly to the worksheet for answers, completing the exercise with little struggle or deep thinking. Students mastered facts, but post-lab assessments showed they were no better at reasoning and applying what they learned in new contexts. Amy was generally pleased with the lesson; she acknowledged it was a little easy for students but did not view it as a significant departure from the approach they had collectively planned.

Round 1 Debrief: Confronting Deep-Seated Practices and Assumptions

A few days later, the group met for a facilitated debrief of their first round of implementation to reflect on video observations and examine student work products. Prior to this meeting, team members individually analyzed selected video episodes from the graphing motion lesson, marking specific time codes and inserting comments to collect observational evidence (see Table 3.2 for an example set of responses). They also had the opportunity to view and study key segments from the other three lessons.

Meeting Summary

Brad initiated the meeting by reviewing the agenda and highlighting three meeting guidelines: (1) comments should reflect the fact that the strategy belongs to the entire team; (2) comments should be grounded in observations of student learning or analysis of student work; (3) each segment of discussion will begin with comments from the presenting teacher. We started the debrief with a thorough discussion and analysis of evidence from the graphing motion lesson and then proceeded with a synopsis, analysis of work samples, and shorter reflective discussion for each of the other three lessons.

As the group revisited their video observations and the rich examples of struggle in the graphing motion lesson (described in the previous section), it opened up a frank discussion about the uneven execution of struggle activities across the first round of implementation. Observational evidence showed that Tom's AP chemistry lesson, much like Jim's, succeeded in getting students to grapple with the concepts of redox, while Ken's chemistry lesson resembled Amy's biology implementation. Much like the student's referencing the lab worksheet on dissolved oxygen (described earlier), Ken's students had too much information prior to the struggle activity and entered the lesson with answers and materials from prior class periods. They had little difficulty with the card sort task and referenced textbooks during the class period when not confident about their answers. Both

■ Table 3.2: Video Analysis Task and Example Comments for Graphing Motion Research Lesson

Lesson Segment and Question Prompt	Marked Time Code Observational Evidence/Comments
Card Sort Activity 00:05:21–00:18:27 Click on the blue time-link below to examine the card sort activity. Mark a few examples where students are clearly "struggling" with the concepts and working to develop an explanation. Elaborate on what you notice. Remember to use your "student lens."	Marked Time: 00:07:59 Don't seem to know dependent vs. independent variable. Marked Time: 00:13:36 "We have no idea . . ." clueless at this point, apparently. Marked Time: 00:15:13 Girl in foreground seems pretty intimidated by the process, worried about not "getting it right" . . . but so far she has not really participated in the sorting process. Marked Time: 00:18:14 Two of the girls are active in sorting the graphs, but the one is still a bystander.
Student Presentations Click on the blue time-links below to examine the students' whiteboard presentations. Mark times and comment on student conceptions and misconceptions that surfaced during the presentations. Dance Fever 00:25:48–00:27:53 P Day 00:28:30–00:30:14	Marked Time: 00:27:43 I can't tell what the label on the vertical axis of the top graph is supposed to represent . . . time? Does the x/y graph just show the position of the dancers? Time has not been used in the graph. Marked Time: 00:29:38 J said the vertical axis was speed but then gave the units as meters per second squared. The graph would be right for speed, however. Marked Time: 00:30:13 The graph is right for how speed changes (before he opens the chute), but J is confused about how the speed will actually change, saying the speed is slowing down.

(Continued)

■ Table 3.2: (Continued)

Lesson Segment and Question Prompt	Marked Time Code Observational Evidence/Comments
Sweet Little Furry Animal 00:30:42–00:32:34 Remember Your Algebra 00:32:56–00:34:12 Sup? Nothing 00:34:30–00:36:00 Fast Break With the Football 00:36:15–00:37:52	Marked Time: 00:31:44 The graph is wrong, and a distance (y) vs. time (x) would look a lot different. She realizes that there is a problem. . . . The biggest misconceptions seem to relate to what variables should be graphed on which axes. Marked Time: 00:33:43 I'm not sure if I am hearing the problem correctly, but it sounds like the slope should be proportional to y^2/x. What they have graphed looks like a square root function, where y is proportional to the square root of x. Marked Time: 00:37:52 Looks pretty good—they graphed time and distance and matched the specified distance with its time. It also shows an increase in speed toward the end. However, they put time and distance on the wrong axes. . . . Distance depends on time, not vice versa. Marked Time: 00:35:59 They are not clear on what is being graphed on the y axis. . . . One says it is "motion"; the other seems to indicate position; they agree that time is on the x axis.
Reflective Comments	It forced them to think about the ways to measure, describe, and graph motion. Most of the students have had experience graphing in other courses but probably very few, if any, have done much with graphing motion. Just an initial thought . . . maybe it would have been good to give each team two scenarios, one that they all had in common and then another simple but different one. They might have been able to get insight from seeing responses to the same problem they had been trying to understand.

Amy and Ken commented on the contrast between the rich, productive struggle in the physics lesson and the mitigated struggle in their implementation experiences.

Moment of Realization

As Amy reflected on the first round of implementation, she explained that she had been somewhat fearful of leaving students without any guiding framework or assistance with the struggle task, "I think it was fear. . . . I was afraid to let the students struggle, afraid of the frustration they would express." After studying the video of the physics lesson, reflecting on student work, and discussing the impact of struggle on students' long-term retention and conceptual understanding, she developed a new appreciation for dissonance. Toward the end of the debrief meeting, she emphatically stated, "Dissonance is good. It was a strength of the [lesson design]. The confusion was the framework that was necessary to build understanding!"

Ken shared similar insights: "I would do my lesson differently the next time I did it. I would do the timing differently. . . . I would have liked to have had a little more struggle because, as you were discussing, I think that is necessary for learning. . . . I gave them too much guidance or too much opportunity for guidance."

Through this analysis and reflection, teachers confronted a deep-seated assumption that students struggling meant students failing. Both Amy and Ken clearly realized they routinely provided students with too much guidance. This diminished students' opportunities to grapple with concepts and become aware of misconceptions that stood in the way of learning. *But an important question remained:* Would this realization be enough to overcome the persistent cultural routines they had learned and practiced throughout their careers as both students and teachers in traditional science classrooms?

Round 2: A Breakthrough in Productive Struggle

During the ensuing planning discussion, all four teachers demonstrated a renewed commitment to implement the struggle/scaffold script. We again worked to develop instructional plans for each content area, beginning with the AP biology research lesson on osmosis and diffusion. The teachers followed the same storyline of struggle/scaffold steps but revised the approach by replacing the card sort strategy with unique struggle activities specifically tailored for each classroom context. As the team worked to develop the discovery lab on osmosis and diffusion (Amy's classroom), she emphatically asserted her commitment to promote struggle.

> (Holding up a copy of the lab packet) Here is the classic American way of teaching. They give you all the answers in the background information. Here is everything that the kids are supposed to know. That was my fatal flaw in the last lesson . . . and the thing that I have to avoid because I directly exposed them to the right answers the day before. . . . So one thing that I'm definitely not going to do is give this to them.

In the weeks ahead, the group completed preparations for a second round of lessons building on what they learned in the first cycle and revising their approach based on these insights and findings. In this second round, all four lessons, including AP biology (Amy) and chemistry (Ken), succeeded in engaging students with very challenging discovery labs. We summarize these two lessons below as prominent examples of the shifts in practice we observed in the second round of implementation.

AP Biology Research Lesson: Productive Struggle With Osmosis and Diffusion

In the AP biology research lesson, students struggled with the concepts of osmosis and diffusion as they worked to design their own procedures and conduct an experiment for placing dialysis bags into five unknown concentrations of sugar water. The objective was to discover the relative concentrations of sugar water in their dialysis bags to the concentrations of the sugar water in their cups. Each of the groups had a different concentration in their dialysis bags, so they were all working on different variations of the same experiment.

Unlike the previous lesson implementation, Amy's students had no prior knowledge about the lab and no reference materials to rely on. There was significant distress in many groups as they struggled to understand the concepts without any assistance from other resources. Amy circulated to clarify instructions and encourage further inquiry but completely suspended verbal guidance, even as students playfully accused her of trying to "lower their grades." Her response was, "You have to learn to live with a little dissonance. It's going to be OK." Rather than giving answers, she asked probing questions like, "Do you think the molarity of the bag might change as it's soaking in the sugar water?" or "Why are you measuring the cups?" When a student asked if they were "on the right track," she smiled and responded with, "It's the joy of discovery; don't you think? . . . Have you set up a data table to collect your data?"

Amy also intentionally carried a notepad to record notes as she circulated among groups. Rather than prematurely interject remarks and provide too much guidance or information, she wrote down various observations, such as misconceptions that individual students had or common patterns of difficulty to address in future instruction. At times, she would look down and pretend to record comments, even though she was intently listening to what students were saying, to encourage them to rely more on their own collective reasoning. In this way, she learned how to foster rigorous levels of inquiry, requiring students to persist with challenging concepts and identify gaps in understanding. The insights she gained enabled her to address these gaps more effectively during post-lab discussion and presentations. She concluded the lesson with a creative illustration on the board, using transparent tape, clear, reclosable plastic bags, and large, dotted cards (representing moles of sucrose) to summarize the experiment and solidify concepts of osmosis and diffusion. She then assigned a series of essay prompts that required students to transfer these concepts to the human body.

Chemistry Lesson: Productive Struggle With Atomic Structure

The chemistry lesson involved a struggle activity with bags containing three different colors of beans that represented the three subatomic particles. Each group of students received several bags and began to circulate throughout the room to trade with other groups and to find bags that represented isotopes of an element.

In stark contrast to Ken's first lesson implementation, this second struggle activity was quite challenging for the class. He did not give students any information for the activity prior to the lesson, and they did not have access to any reference materials during the class period. One student voiced her frustration with the new approach by exclaiming, "I can't believe you're making us do this. I don't understand this." Ken calmly encouraged her to keep working on the task but continued to suspend verbal guidance or telling. He also effectively implemented the activity so that groups were all working on different aspects of a larger problem and could not simply copy the answers from other groups. At the end of class, he asked students to use the information to calculate the average atomic mass for the given elements. In a subsequent lesson, Ken discussed the activity with the class, worked through key misconceptions, and later assigned a transfer prompt requiring students to explain how these bags and beans were an accurate or inaccurate representation of the concepts.

Round 2 Debrief: Celebrating Change

For the second round of lessons, team members individually analyzed selected video episodes from the osmosis and diffusion research lesson and again logged time codes and comments to collect observational evidence (see Table 3.3) prior to our face-to-face debrief session.

Meeting Summary

The second debrief followed the same format as the first cycle with a review of guidelines, extended analysis of the research lesson (osmosis and diffusion), and shorter reflective discussions on each of the other three discovery labs.

A tone of collective celebration characterized the meeting as we discussed video observations from each implementation. In addition to the episodes of productive struggle observed in Amy and Ken's implementation efforts (described in the previous section), both the AP chemistry (Tom) and physics (Jim) discovery labs also showed evidence of significant struggle with challenging scientific tasks. In fact, Tom explained this was the first time in more than 30 years of teaching that he observed students design their own experimental procedures. He was gratified to see students embrace such deep inquiry and scientific analysis.

A New Level of Inquiry for Students

Building on this observational evidence, group members shared promising results from student work samples as well as informal student interviews. Amy shared convincing evidence from the transfer prompt she had assigned, explaining that within one class of AP Biology students, there were 10 different approaches to the same transfer question, and all but one student demonstrated an advanced conceptual understanding of osmosis and diffusion. Jim reported progress on pre- and post-assessments in physics where students showed improved scientific reasoning. Other members shared evidence from informal interviews with students who indicated that they "learned things better this way," "had a better understanding," or "enjoyed having the chance to solve problems."

■ **Table 3.3: Video Analysis Task and Example Comments for Osmosis and Diffusion Research Lesson**

Lesson Segment and Question Prompt	Marked Time Code Observational Evidence/Comments
Discovery Lab Click on the blue time-links below to examine the discovery lab. Mark examples where students are clearly "struggling" with the concepts. Elaborate on what you notice. Remember to use your "student lens." 00:00:00–00:06:21 00:06:21–00:13:48 00:13:48–00:20:42 00:20:42–00:32:49	Marked Time: 00:13:40 In this first section, there are several instances of struggle. . . . first group not sure how to measure molarity . . . J is not sure how to measure grams of solute. A knows the water moves, which leads them to mass the changes. . . . They are measuring the cups but they aren't sure why– C is completely lost. J's head hurts; they are NOT having fun, and they [want to know] if they are on the right track. . . . The second group starts off completely confused . . . not sure what to do. M is laughing at the guys . . . Z gets it. K suggests using food coloring to track the movement of water. B & M think sugar is moving. K & Z get it first . . . and understand the bags will gain and lose weight according to the osmosis.
White Board Presentations and Scaffolding Activity Click on the blue time-links below to examine the students' whiteboard presentations. 1) Mark times and comment on student conceptions and misconceptions that are surfaced during the presentations.	Marked Time: 00:39:40 They've figured the correct movement of water! Their logic is pretty good for picking between .6 and .8, admitting that the bags were leaking. Marked Time: 00:44:19 "Highest weight had highest molarity???" Had them in descending order. . . . G weighed these things multiple times.

(Continued)

■ Table 3.3: (Continued)

Lesson Segment and Question Prompt	Marked Time Code Observational Evidence/Comments
2) Also, mark some specific examples from the lesson which suggest students were discovering misconceptions and developing new understandings.	Marked Time: 00:59:10
	They are lost! Z said it correctly, but his group isn't understanding or helping. "I don't know where our data is!" Data . . . missing.
	Marked Time: 01:01:11
	We measured % error—B isn't sure what they measured. . . . We figured the one that changed the least would be the one with 1.0 molarity because . . .
If you are short on time, just choose 3 or 4 of these time-links to study. Be sure to watch the closing segment where index cards and plastic bags are used to illustrate the concepts.	Marked Time: 01:02:06
	R: "We never discussed what the data meant."
	They all blame each other . . . then C describes the sugar sitting at the bottom . . .
	They figured out that they didn't stir the stock solution, and explained . . .
Group 1 00:38:42–00:42:46	Marked Time: 01:08:35
	B tells the truth. They mixed up the bags and didn't know what bag was what.
Group 2 00:42:46–00:52:19	Marked Time: 01:09:54
	Z figured out that all the starting weights were equal . . .
Group 3 00:52:19–00:58:11	Marked Time: 01:10:58
	K's face tells his confusion, admits "no idea."
Group 4 00:58:11–01:00:58	Marked Time: 01:11:53
	E and G knew that the least amount of change would reveal the identity of the bag.
Group 5 01:00:58–01:09:36	Marked Time: 01:12:30
Closing Illustration 01:09:36–01:12:33	This is an excellent realization activity.
Reflective Comments	. . . through the struggle with the lab, more personal learning happened. Students were able to internalize the information more than if given a "cookbook" lab. . . . The internal struggle is essential to build deep understanding or at least a platform for deeper understanding.

As we synthesized evidence and recorded successes and failures of the struggle/scaffold efforts, all members voiced interest in further refining this approach with future inquiry projects. Ken suggested it might be interesting to schedule struggle/scaffold lessons at strategic points in the curriculum. Tom talked about designing more discovery labs to observe and assist students' progress with planning scientific procedures. Jim suggested the possibility of including a journaling component during the struggle stage to help students reflect more meaningfully on their own thought processes. Amy proposed a related idea of creating assignments where students are graded for the process and not for their results.

A New Level of Inquiry for Teachers

In addition to observations of student growth in inquiry, the team discussed how lesson study had enlightened their own understanding of the teacher role in facilitating learning of science. Teachers learned to better differentiate productive struggle from failure and to tailor instructional moves accordingly. They began to recognize how such teacher decisions as the materials they chose to provide or the comments they might interject during lab activities can significantly influence the depth of student learning. They started teaching the importance of error analysis by allowing students to experience the consequences of imprecise measurement procedures. They learned to monitor group projects more purposefully, making sure the struggle resulted from challenging problem-solving tasks, not from confusion with instructions, frustration with group dynamics, or lack of teacher support. And they patiently helped students discover the satisfaction that comes from persisting with a difficult task.

Six months later, after a sustained effort to incorporate these new teaching practices, Amy sent an e-mail to share some positive assessment results, which she described as "higher than any class ever before." She went on to explain,

> I am so happy for my students, I just sat down, closed the door of my office and cried and cried and gave thanks. I have to believe I changed the way I taught, that making them struggle really bridged the gap. This was my most enjoyable year of teaching in my 28 years . . . Amy

Final Reflections

This case study illustrates how a group of U.S. teachers can learn with and from each other through thoughtful and persistent study of teaching.

While several team members initially reverted back to more familiar instructional routines that minimized student discomfort, these same teachers altered their practice in the second iteration of lessons to foster rich and challenging struggle opportunities for students. This change in practice allowed teachers to observe and record specific student misconceptions, which they helped students recognize and address in subsequent lesson activities.

Investing in this kind of sustained effort to openly study and refine their teaching required a substantial amount of trust and willingness to become vulnerable, as Jim communicated in his reflections on the process.

> I had a subtle thought when we began . . . a little bit of fear of being exposed or something like that. But, I figured I'll go ahead and take a chance. In the end, I think that was probably the best thing about it. You could discuss and find common things that we struggle with, and common things that we're successful with, and new ways of doing things that you see from your colleagues . . . things that just don't come up in casual conversation. It's not going to take place unless you really mean for it to take place. . . . It's an extremely positive and heartening experience.

Amy shared similar reflections about overcoming initial anxieties:

> I was completely and totally terrified. . . . I thought, "What if I blow it?" And then I thought, "Who cares? We're going to focus on student learning and we just want to study this. Let's put my money where my mouth is and let's do it." And it was so rewarding.

Ken expressed amazement at how well the process worked with experienced teachers and how much we all have to learn "even if we've been teaching for 25 years."

Conditions That Enabled Collaborative Improvement

During the final reflection meeting, teachers also shared thoughts and observations about conditions that made it possible to openly work on their practice and learn from each other in ways they had not previously experienced. In this closing section, we combine the team's observations with our own analysis and suggestions for replicating these conditions in

U.S. schools (elementary or secondary). Our analysis covers four essential conditions: stable settings, facilitated inquiry, recursive process focused on improving teaching, and reflective observation of lessons.

Stable Settings

Settings are "any instance in which two or more people come together in new relationships over a sustained period of time in order to achieve certain goals" (Sarason, 1972, p. 1). Although many schools have faculty meetings and department and/or grade-level meetings, these are typically usurped by bureaucratic, operational, social, and personnel matters and do not function as stable settings focused on teaching and learning. This high school case study was no exception.

Since there were no existing settings in place for collaborative inquiry, teachers creatively mapped out a schedule, agreeing on specific times each month where they could repurpose other meetings or carve out time for collective lesson study work within the contracted day. This resulted in 22 hours of meeting time strategically distributed across the year. Once the calendar of meetings was established and published, they shared it with the principal, who also played a key role in supporting and protecting this setting from other distractions and commitments.

Options for Securing Settings

This task becomes exponentially more complicated when faced with the challenge of creating new settings for a school-wide inquiry program, with dedicated time for individual workgroups to meet three or four times a month. This plays out differently in various schools and districts.

For some schools, it's a matter of repurposing settings that already exist. This presents challenges for reclaiming settings that may have a history of unproductive meetings (see Chapter 6 for two examples) or displacing other tasks that still need to be accomplished at other times (see "Organizing Settings Chart" in Chapter 5).

For other schools, the task requires carving out new settings within the school day dedicated to collaborative inquiry and instructional improvement. This presents challenges for adjusting bell schedules, aligning conference periods, and potentially securing buy-in from various stakeholders (teachers' union, board members, parents, etc.). Some options we have observed include the following:

- Arrange teaching schedules so that grade-level or subject-area teams share a *common planning time or conference period* one or more days per week.
- Have core subject teachers meet during physical education or psychomotor periods.
- Create a *combo calendar* for collaborative inquiry, merging various settings at strategic points across the year (e.g., segments of pupil-free in-service days, contracted days before or after the school year; monthly grade-level or department meetings; etc.).
- Establish a weekly *early-release* day (typically elementary schools) or weekly *late-start* day (more typical for secondary schools) by lengthening the bell schedule by a few minutes on other school days.
- Schedule *after-school meetings* (where permitted by contract regulations). Some districts or schools have established teacher contracts with an allotted number of meetings per month; others make it voluntary and generate interest through word of mouth and peer recruitment. In a few cases, schools have secured funding to provide modest stipends or additional compensation.

Protecting and Supporting Settings

Regardless of how time is secured, what's more important is ensuring settings are protected, focused, and supported. This requires a mutual commitment from teachers and administrators. Establishing settings for teacher teams should always be considered in concert with corresponding support settings for team facilitators and instructional leaders. Chapter 5 covers this in detail, including a comprehensive framework for cascading layers of settings, leadership, and assistance.

Facilitated Inquiry

In this case study, not only was the setting stable and protected, but it was also carefully facilitated so that meetings were connected over time and productively structured to guide subsequent phases of inquiry. This involved a delicate balance between the detailed structures of lesson study and the freedom to think creatively about teaching. As Jim emphasized in our reflection meeting:

> There's also an element to the way that this worked that I think is an important element . . . that you provided us with structure but also gave us an incredible amount of freedom. And you treated us with respect as professionals and you looked to us to

be developers. There's a certain response that you get when that's the case and I think that's a critical element. . . . If something like this is planned as an extension or continuation, that part cannot be ignored.

Having a facilitator with deep knowledge of lesson study and an organized plan for each meeting freed the group to focus on teaching and learning rather than on negotiating agendas and priorities. As the project progressed, this engendered confidence that meetings would be highly relevant, well organized, and a good use of teachers' time.

Trained Facilitators

Our experience with this project demonstrated that even motivated and productive teams require facilitation to maximize the collaborative inquiry experience. Each team needs a trained leader dedicated to guiding the process, moderating discussion, probing for deeper understanding, and providing a balance of structure and support.

Replicating this effect beyond one case study team requires an important shift from the external expert leading a single group to a campus-wide, distributed leadership model where the outside expert and administrators identify and support teacher leaders to perform the facilitator role. This distributed approach has benefits for teachers, administrators, and content specialists.

First, teacher facilitators are uniquely positioned to build rapport with colleagues and guide the inquiry process as a full participant, identifying immediate applications for the classroom as they work alongside group members. They also assist the group to remain focused over time as other projects or responsibilities compete for teachers' time and attention.

Second, the use of teacher facilitators frees up coaches and content specialists (when available) to play the role of knowledgeable resource rather than team leader. This reduces chances of the setting being converted from inquiry-focused to a more conventional professional development presentation that puts teachers in a passive rather than active role.

Finally, raising up teacher facilitators also means assisting administrators to adopt new roles as instructional leaders with a sustained focus on supporting implementation and building capacity for inquiry (as we describe in Chapter 5).

Attributes of Successful Facilitators

When selecting a teacher facilitator to lead the inquiry process, some key attributes to look for include the following:

Willingness to lead

- Sufficient bandwidth and commitment to prioritize facilitation work
- Willing to be trained and guide teachers through the inquiry process
- Reflective, self-critical, and committed to lifelong learning

Ability to help a group work together productively

- Respected by colleagues, a good listener, and patient with the learning of others; able to build consensus when there are differences of opinion
- Able to help a group follow through, stay focused on instruction, and get things done
- Able to grasp and articulate the inquiry process (with support and training)

Organizational skills

- Takes responsibility for preparing agendas, sending out reminders, and keeping a record of plans between meetings
- Effectively manages electronic files and resources

Launching a Pilot Project

When starting lesson study or collaborative inquiry for the first time, choosing a facilitator is also a critical factor in identifying a pilot team (or teams). For guidance on preparing for a pilot project, see the "Pilot Team Selection Inventory" on the companion website (http://www.corwin.com/ErmelingTeachingBetter).

Recursive Process Focused on Improving Teaching

The structure of the inquiry process itself was another important factor in the science group's success. Like our experience in Japan, a subtle but critical aspect of lesson study was how the jointly developed research lesson became the central unit of analysis. This emphasis on *teaching* rather than the *teacher* helped promote a sense of experimentation and openness to discovery, as opposed to the more guarded and defensive stance typical of contexts focused on teacher evaluation.

Equally subtle and important was the recursive nature of the process. After completing initial implementation and discovering deep-seated practices that were mitigating opportunities for struggle, teachers had the opportunity to repeat the process and make important instructional adjustments. This helped the group move from interesting insights to actual changes in practice and persevere with the problem long enough to achieve tangible student results. In the excerpt that follows, the teachers summarize their experience with the process and highlight the importance of follow-through as a catalyst for changes in teaching:

Amy: It's really what professional development is in my mind. It's the best kind of in-service that anybody could have. It's what really changes teaching.

Tom: We're not just getting general principles from education or science.

Jim: And you try them and analyze them. It's not just like, "Do this" and you forget and you might do it. . . . You follow up.

Amy: And it doesn't matter that . . . you teach chemistry, and that you teach physics, and I teach biology. We have very common ground to talk.

Inquiry-Based Protocols

For the facilitation of this group, and other groups we've supported in subsequent projects, use of clearly specified *protocols* has played a key role in formalizing this recursive, inquiry-based process. First of all, protocols help to ensure that each group's work adheres to the essential features of instructional inquiry while at the same time enabling adaptations for local context and immediate instructional needs. Second, for members within a single group, but also for school-wide or district-wide implementation efforts, protocols help build coherence by establishing a common process and shared language of inquiry. Third, when carefully tested and derived from an authentic context, protocols can help nurture critical inquiry skills and reflective dispositions, as described in Chapter 2 (fashioning a coherent storyline, articulating and testing hypotheses, relying on evidence to guide reflection, embracing collective ownership of improvement, and persisting with problems over time).

Finally, protocols help to provide much-needed focus and continuity typically absent in site-based collaborative settings, which are often riddled with distractions. They equip the facilitator with simple tools for maintaining joint productive activity, keeping the emphasis on instruction, and holding the group accountable to collect feedback on the effects of their teaching.

Choosing a Protocol

Numerous authors and organizations have developed protocols to guide teacher collaboration and instructional improvement efforts. Whether working on lesson study or other forms of collaborative instructional inquiry, the key criteria for choosing an effective inquiry protocol include the following:

Are the tasks, steps, and accompanying resources (templates and tools) sufficiently outlined and specified?

Does it focus on the study of teaching and learning: planning, implementing, and reflecting on lessons in relationship to evidence from observations or student work products?

Does it focus on collective ownership of teaching rather than critiquing individual teachers?

Does it feature a recursive process enabling teachers to persist with improvement of teaching over time?

Has it been tested and refined through research and development with a variety of school contexts and teams?

Example protocols that meet the effectiveness criteria (listed in alphabetical order):

Lewis and Hurd (2011) handbook and protocols for lesson study: http://www.lessonresearch.net/books1.html

The Talking Teaching Network's PDAR (Plan, Do, Analyze, Reflect) protocol (Saunders & Marcelletti, 2015): http://www.talkingteaching.org/teacher-collaboration-handbook

Singer (2015) protocol for Observational Inquiry (OI): http://www.corwin.com/books/Book241059

Observing and Reflecting on Lessons

Pros and Cons of Video

A final critical component in this team's experience was the opportunity to watch research lessons unfold in the classroom and observe colleagues implement the jointly developed instructional plans. Substituting video for live observation offered both advantages and disadvantages for the lesson study process. On the positive side, it uniquely enabled teachers to "slow down" teaching, pause, rewind, record comments, and study episodes more than once as needed.

The preserved comments and corresponding time codes were valuable resources, both before and during the debrief meeting, assisting the group to rely on evidence for reflective commentary and discussions. From a logistical standpoint, the use of video allowed for more flexible scheduling of lesson observations without the need for coordinating schedules and arranging substitutes to cover classes.

However, it also presented several important constraints. Most significantly, the teachers were limited to a single viewing angle rather than distributing themselves throughout the room to capture data and interactions from all students. The time delay between lesson and face-to-face debrief reduced the clarity of memory and freshness of observations, even though we had access to the video recording. There were also limitations in capturing quality audio with overlapping talk during student group work and pair conversations. In addition, the process of capturing and preparing videos for analysis required both time and technical capacity not readily available in all schools and districts.

Live observation supplemented by video analysis would likely provide the best combination of data collection and reflection opportunities, but considering limitations with teachers' time and schedules, the use of video proved to be an acceptable substitute. While not as powerful as live observations, it still enabled teachers to "see" the lessons unfold in the classroom, rather than simply discuss results in the abstract.

The Power of Seeing the Lesson

As introduced in the beginning of this chapter with the image of the Japanese toothpick, it was this experience of seeing a tangible demonstration of something different and effective that inspired self-reflection for the group and created the circumstances for change. In a post-project questionnaire, both Amy and Ken identified the video analysis opportunities as a primary influence on their changes in practice between the first and second iteration of lessons. Watching the video of Jim's lesson on graphing motion helped remove a veil restricting their reflective process. It created a contrast by which to view their own instruction and illuminated the missing element of struggle in their

Conditions That Enabled Collaborative Improvement

1. Stable settings
2. Facilitated inquiry
3. Recursive process focused on improving teaching
4. Observing and reflecting on lessons

own classrooms. As Amy articulated during a moment of insight, "It came alive in a way that I had never heard before in the classroom." This was the key that expanded their horizons of practice and propelled the group forward into the next cycle of planning and implementation.

Conclusion

The results from this science case study provide a distinct example of change and expanded horizons, but it's equally important not to overgeneralize from this example. Our observations with numerous other lesson study and collaborative inquiry projects demonstrate that at least some of this group's success was likely attributable to the unique circumstances of a pilot project. Advantages included self-selected volunteers, direct facilitation from outside experts, and immediate access to a strong alternative example from a fellow team member (Jim's prior experience with implementing productive struggle). The next two chapters explain why these conditions and results can be difficult to replicate at scale, even in the most high-functioning contexts, and propose several specific strategies for addressing this important challenge.

REFLECTION QUESTIONS

KEY PRINCIPLE: *"Seeing that something can be completely different is one of the most effective ways of opening eyes to the ubiquity of cultural practices and creating the circumstances for change"* (Gallimore & Stigler, 2003, p. 27).

1. What are some of the conditions that helped the science team see something different? How might you create those conditions in your context?

2. Reflect on the collaborative settings in your school. Is there sufficient time protected for instructional improvement? How confident are teachers that this time will be well structured and uninterrupted?

3. In the story of the science team, what might have happened if they ended the project after one cycle of implementation? Why is it important to have a recursive process? Why is it important to focus on teaching instead of the teacher?

ADDITIONAL RESOURCES

- See Leader's Guide in the Appendix for additional team exercises from this chapter and presentation ideas for the "Japanese Toothpick (*Tsumayōji*)."
- Visit the companion website to download presentation slides, including a full color digital image of the portrait. Also find customizable templates, checklists, and tools to assist your implementation efforts.

Available at http://www.corwin.com/ErmelingTeachingBetter

REFERENCES

Bransford, J. D., Brown, A. L., & Cocking, R. R. (2000). *How people learn: Brain, mind, experience, and school* (Expanded ed.). Washington DC: National Academy Press.

Gallimore, R. (1996). Classrooms are just another cultural activity. In D. L. Speece & B. K. Keogh (Eds.), *Research on classroom ecologies: Implications for inclusion of children with learning disabilities* (pp. 229–250). Mahwah, NJ: Erlbaum.

Gallimore, R., & Stigler, J. (2003). Closing the teaching gap: Assisting teachers to adapt to changing standards and assessments. In C. Richardson (Ed.), *Whither assessment?* (pp. 25–36). London, England: Qualifications and Curriculum Authority.

Haskell, R. E. (2001). *Transfer of learning: cognition, instruction, and reasoning.* San Diego, CA: Academic Press.

Hutchins, E. (1993). Learning to navigate. In S. Chaiklin & J. Lave (Eds.), *Understanding practice: Perspectives on activity and context* (pp. 35–63). Cambridge, England: Cambridge University Press.

Lewis, C., & Hurd, J. (2011). *Lesson study step by step: How teacher learning communities improve instruction.* Portsmouth, NH: Heinemann.

Sarason, S. (1972). *The creation of settings and the future societies.* San Francisco, CA: Jossey-Bass.

Saunders, W., & Marcelletti, D. (2015). *Teacher collaboration handbook.* Los Angeles, CA: Talking Teaching Network.

Singer, T. W. (2015). *Opening doors to equity: A practical guide to observation-based professional learning.* Thousand Oaks, CA: Corwin.

Wellington, J., & Osborne, J. (2001). *Language and literacy in science education.* Philadelphia, PA: Open University Press.

This chapter was adapted from previously published work in the following:

Ermeling, B. A. (2010). Tracing the effects of teacher inquiry on classroom practice. *Teaching and Teacher Education, 26*(3), 377–388.

Ermeling, B. A., & Gallimore, R. (2014/2015). Close to practice learning. From the December 2014/January 2015 online version of *Educational Leadership, 72*(4). Alexandria, VA: ASCD. ©2014 by ASCD. Adapted with permission. Learn more at http://www.ascd.org.

CHAPTER

4

Deepening Knowledge

Why Expansive Change Is Difficult and What We Might Do About It

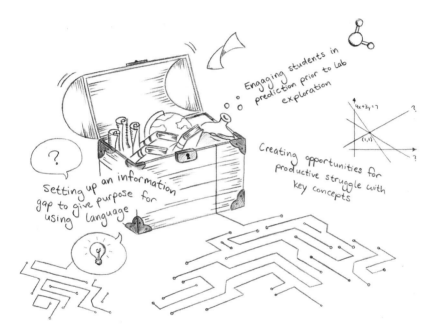

Virtual Treasure Chest

Engaging students in prediction prior to lab exploration

Creating opportunities for productive struggle with key concepts

Setting up an information gap to give purpose for using language

---

KEY PRINCIPLE

Hard-won assets of local knowledge should be diligently pursued, continually refined, and globally shared.

Painting by high school student artist, Emily Tam, 2015. ©2015 Brad & Genevieve Ermeling.

While the improvements reported in the science case study (Chapter 3) are noteworthy, there is a major caveat—changes like this are extremely difficult to replicate at scale. In a number of contexts, we've observed schools that improved teaching and student achievement by implementing well-functioning teacher teams, but most of these teams made only modest changes to instructional approaches already in use. We saw little evidence of expanded instructional practices like those the science team experienced.

For example, in one middle school that won an award for exemplary collaborative practice, a team of algebra teachers diligently worked to improve teaching of mathematical procedures. They were collegial, punctual, efficient in their use of time, and clearly committed to the process. Yet, research observations of this team and other secondary schools in the same project showed few signs that even high-functioning teams were interested, willing, or able to raise the bar and move beyond teaching procedures to focus on better teaching of mathematical connections and concepts. What follows are some recorded observations researchers preserved from the algebra team at the award-winning site.

Evidence of high-functioning collaboration included the following:

- Group demonstrated excellent attendance.
- Facilitator was adequately prepared, including providing and following an agenda.
- Facilitator made an effort to include all group members in the conversation.
- Group members showed willingness to try using an instructional manipulative.
- All members of the group were committed to teaching the lesson to their students.

Evidence of limitations in instructional improvement included the following:

- Learning goals for jointly planned lessons were procedural (e.g., multiplication of binomials) and lacked any description of what students should understand about the underlying mathematical concept (e.g., the distributive property as the basis for all multiplication algorithms).
- Group's planning did not include a discussion of students' current knowledge or understanding, or a discussion of what students should understand about the concept.

- Teacher-created examples were problematic and were not worked out prior to teaching the lesson. This led to wasted time during the lesson and confusion for students.
- Lesson incorporated a mathematical manipulative with which teachers were only slightly familiar.
- Group did not explore or discuss how the manipulative related to the concept being studied or how the use of the manipulative would facilitate student learning.
- Both successful and unsuccessful aspects of the lesson were attributed to the use of the manipulative (Thompson & Stigler, 2008, p. 4).

These examples are typical of what we observed for other math teams at the middle school as well as other secondary schools across the district. In fact, analysis of teams' work products at the middle school showed that, although each identified goals for what students should understand or be able to do, none of the teams specified a conceptual learning goal. Genevieve documented similar findings at one of the district high schools, where a math department successfully stabilized settings for five teacher teams, but discussions about instruction in all five groups were rudimentary and focused on similar procedural goals (Graff-Ermeling, 2007).

Why Expansive Change Is So Difficult

One underlying reason these more expansive and durable changes in teaching are rarely observed is that "teaching is a cultural activity" learned over time through participation in deeply rooted cultural settings and routines (Gallimore, 1996; Hiebert et al., 2003; Hiebert, Gallimore, & Stigler, 2002; Stigler & Hiebert, 1999, p. 11). Practicing and perfecting procedures, for example, has been identified by researchers as a pervasive cultural script for U.S. math instruction. This was, undoubtedly, how the algebra teachers at the middle school experienced math instruction throughout their K–20 school careers. The teachers perfected the procedural teaching script well enough to see modest increases in test scores but did not recognize the limits of this approach on students' conceptual understanding.

Little (2003) describes how teacher communities' out-of-classroom interactions can "both open up and close off opportunities" for learning and reflective practice (p. 939). Illustrating her point with specific transcript excerpts, she raises the concern "that formation of tightly bounded professional communities with their specialized language and stock of familiar classroom stories . . . might result in highly isolated and insular groups . . .

replacing the isolated classroom teacher with the isolated teacher group" (p. 939.) Teacher teams then, just as individual teachers, are constrained by the insular nature of their practice, both in their limited access to research and expertise in content knowledge for their discipline, and in their conceptions of how that content might be effectively taught.

Addressing the Problem

What might assist teacher teams from setting low ceilings on their efforts to improve instruction? In this chapter (and the next), we explore several possibilities.

1. Move away from "best practices."

2. Deepen professional knowledge through inquiry-based digital libraries.

3. Develop professional judgment needed to deliver timely and effective instruction.

4. Adopt a new framework for leadership, settings, and assistance (see Chapter 5).

Move Away From "Best Practices"

One reason we seldom observed teams make significant changes in teaching is because of the pervasive U.S. emphasis on "best practices," which discourage rather than encourage the continuous improvement of instruction. *Best* suggests a definitive superiority to alternative practices; it's a label based more on an appeal to authority than on research. As an iterative process of ongoing exploration and testing, research avoids definitive statements like *best practices*. At the very least, a claim of best practice needs to include caveats and a detailed accounting of the circumstances in which it was—and wasn't—effective. Instead, best practices are typically defined in ways that create three big problems.

Best Practices Encourage a Plug-and-Play Approach

Teachers are encouraged to adopt new methods and use them as often as possible, but they're not often provided opportunities to analyze or develop knowledge about those methods. For example, in the district where we observed the award-winning algebra team, many professional development providers and math specialists had been pushing greater use of conceptually rich mathematical problems. *Rich problems* or *concept tasks* had received the best practice label on the basis, in part, of the mistaken conclusion that higher-achieving countries teach a greater number of rich problems than the United States does.

In fact, the number of conceptual problems in U.S. eighth grade algebra lessons is comparable to what higher-performing countries offer. This was a key finding from the TIMSS, in which researchers looked at hundreds of lesson videos randomly collected in seven countries. The crucial difference wasn't the number of conceptual problems but *how* teachers presented the problems. In higher-performing countries, teachers taught rich problems as they were intended to be taught—conceptually. Japanese teachers, for example, might introduce a new concept by providing students with opportunities to grapple with novel problems and challenging mathematical tasks *before* teaching specific formulas or procedures (see a detailed example later in this chapter).

In contrast, in each of the 83 U.S. classroom videos in the TIMSS, teachers converted challenging problems into procedural tasks by front-loading lessons with specific formulas and rules that students could use to find right answers (Hiebert et al., 2005). Rich problems require more detailed, content-rich instructional planning and execution than U.S. teachers typically are trained to engage in. There's little emphasis in U.S. curricula on how or when teachers should teach various problems to facilitate students getting the "why"—true mathematical learning and understanding.

So simply plugging in rich problems—without changing the underlying instruction—is a form of practice that doesn't deserve the adjective *best.* Instead of improving instructional methods, all it does is reinforce the decades-old U.S. instructional methods documented in the TIMSS and confirmed by our observations at the award-winning middle school. It implies that each practice works perfectly without instructional development or change on the part of teachers. It treats teaching as a simple collection of independent and replaceable parts. But teaching is far more complicated than that. Teachers need time to learn new practices; time to help students respond to them; and time to configure, adapt, and incorporate these practices into classroom instruction.

Best Practices Uncouple Learning Goals From Instructional Methods

Good teaching must always be associated with a well-defined learning goal. A good teaching method for one learning goal might not be effective for another. Without specifying learning goals, there's no way to sort out which teaching methods are better than others.

One of the goals for the eighth grade students at the award-winning middle school was high performance on a district periodic assessment that contained a number of mathematical procedures students had to execute correctly. Research has shown that a good way to prepare students for recalling facts or procedures is repeated, error-free practice with immediate feedback.

Another learning goal the algebra teachers discussed for these same eighth graders was not just to perform well on the unit test but also to remember these procedures for the rest of the year and be able to modify them to solve slightly different problems that will come up in the future. Research has shown that this kind of learning goal is better achieved if students are required to exert some intellectual effort in making sense of the procedures, perhaps wrestling with the question of why the procedures work (Clark & Bjork, 2014; Hiebert & Grouws, 2007). These two different learning goals are better achieved by two different teaching methods. That's why encouraging teachers to plug in a supposed best practice is not only misguided but also can stymie students' long-term learning and achievement.

For this reason it's better to replace the misleading term *best practice* with *effective practices,* each explicitly tied to a well-defined learning goal. Labeling any teaching method as *best* stops the ongoing search for better approaches and prevents teachers and researchers from continually working to improve instruction. In fact, the question of which teaching method is best might not even be researchable. The better question is this: For this learning objective, for this group of students, at this point in the academic year, what might be some promising practices to try out, refine, and try again?

Best Practices Focus on Activity Instead of Achievement

In many school contexts, the idea of sharing best practices represents a search for ways to keep the classroom environment lively and stimulating. This was also part of the algebra team's discussion at the award-winning middle school. In this context, *best* is sometimes labeled *fresh, innovative,* or *high interest.* Although there's nothing wrong with employing high-interest activities, it's counterproductive to make them a focal point and primary objective of instruction rather than a means of fostering student learning of specific content and skills. Ends can be confused with means; activities can be substituted for achievement.

Introducing new technologies is a prime example. Thousands of districts and schools have adopted one-to-one initiatives with new laptops or mobile devices and introduced interactive whiteboards, assessment clickers, and software applications, all of which are potentially powerful tools. But (as noted in Chapter 1) without careful planning and training, these devices and resources can quickly become expensive and colorful accessories for existing instructional methods—and one more reason teachers may not be focused on planning, reflecting, and teaching.

The same narrative describes popular best practices, such as problem-based learning, cooperative groups, or hands-on activities and manipulatives like those observed at the award-winning middle school. As the research report noted, teachers "did not explore or discuss how the manipulative related to the concept being studied or how the use of the manipulative would facilitate student learning" (Thompson & Stigler, 2008, p. 4).

Gravitating toward the latest and greatest ideas with hopes of keeping students on task, interested, and engaged is not a bad thing. These can be effective instructional approaches—for certain learning objectives. But that nuance often is ignored, so teachers don't receive the training or aren't given the time to learn how to leverage these new approaches to foster student learning and understanding.

Similarly, observations of classroom teaching often mistake the mere presence of specific instructional practices as meaningful rather than attending to whether students are learning something. Did the teacher use higher-order questioning in the lesson? Yes or no? How many times? It would be better to ask: When the teacher used higher-order questioning, did it create a powerful learning opportunity? Or perhaps an even more important question would be: Was the lesson planned and executed so students had challenging learning opportunities that higher-order questioning enabled?

Deepen Professional Knowledge

Another reason we seldom observed teams move out of their comfort range is aptly described by the truism "we don't know what we don't know." For example, mathematics teachers at the award-winning middle school seemed to have too little knowledge of mathematics to recognize they were limiting their scope of improvement by focusing only on better teaching of procedures. They were thrilled and satisfied that their collaborative improvement efforts had raised student achievement—on procedural mathematics assessments.

It is hardly surprising that their image of effective math instruction narrowly focused on teaching procedures. Applying procedures to problems is what they knew about mathematics. It was the way they were taught throughout their own K–20 school careers. Procedure-based mathematics instruction is so deeply soaked into the culture of American schooling that teachers, administrators, parents, and students take for granted that it is the proper way to teach and the goal of schooling.

Definitions of Knowledge

What kinds of knowledge might be needed to broaden teachers' vision of practice? In addition to content and pedagogical knowledge, Shulman (1986) added a third form he described as pedagogical content knowledge (PCK). PCK is "conceptualized as knowing content in pedagogically useful ways . . . at the intersection of teaching and learning" (Kersting, Givvin, Thompson, Santagata, & Stigler, 2012, p. 570). Another way to describe PCK is *knowing how to make content comprehensible to learners.*

Hiebert et al. (2002) argued that all forms of professional knowledge for teaching—content knowledge, pedagogical knowledge, and PCK—must be tightly integrated to teach a particular lesson well. Such integrated knowledge for teaching is linked with practice and is detailed, concrete, and specific. This differs from research knowledge that tends to be more abstract and disconnected from practice. It also differs from general pedagogical approaches, such as checking for understanding and other instructional devices that are applicable across a wide range of content.

Cochran-Smith and Lytle (1999) distinguish between three conceptions of teacher knowledge. The first is knowledge-*for*-practice: formal knowledge and theory generated by researchers for teacher use. The second is knowledge-*in*-practice: practical knowledge embedded in teachers' daily practice and reflection. And the final conception is knowledge-*of*-practice, which is generated "when teachers treat their own classrooms and schools as sites for intentional investigation at the same time as they treat the knowledge and theory produced by others as generative material for interrogation and interpretation" (p. 250).

Accessing Knowledge

So how might teachers both generate and access integrated, specific knowledge while diligently investigating their practice? A common model is hiring an expert who provides access to knowledge either on site (such as a content coach or curriculum specialist) or through conventional workshops and college courses. However, not every school can afford a coach or specialist, and content mastery does not guarantee coaching skill. Workshops and courses are often too removed from practice, too limited in scope, and focused on general principles, rather than the kind of problem-specific knowledge generated in lesson study and other inquiry-based collaborative models. In addition, these conventional modes of dispensing "knowledge-*for*-practice" do not provide just-in-time access to teacher teams working to adapt and investigate new content and approaches for specific needs and lessons in local classroom contexts.

If we assume that sometime in the future most teachers are part of collaborative teams engaged in continuous improvement, technology might prove a way to deliver just-in-time access to helpful resources that would, for example, deepen knowledge of alternative approaches so that teaching mathematical procedures is not the only goal.

One solution might be video-rich, online digital libraries that teacher teams can easily access while engaged in continuous inquiry. Many kinds of libraries can be imagined: those created by a local school system, a state, a consortium of states, or national research and professional organizations. Organizations with a research and experience base might begin building such digital libraries while, hopefully, more schools embed inquiry opportunities in teachers' everyday routines.

Imagine inquiry-based digital libraries stocked with rich contextual resources emerging from local contexts—a *virtual treasure chest* for teachers. The libraries could include thoughtfully developed inquiry reports, project summaries, practitioner narratives, or detailed case studies captured in various forms of media (visual displays, written text, videos, pictures, or diagrams). Each project or case study could be accompanied by multiple resources, such as lesson videos, lesson plans, teacher analysis, commentary, and interpretation of each lesson; well-specified learning goals and formative assessments for monitoring progress and providing feedback; alternative instructional moves for creating learning opportunities to address specific student needs; and links to resources for deepening knowledge of subject-matter content. Lesson videos could also include links to specific segments and commentary to stimulate inquiry and discussion. Not a few examples, and not just those produced by "stars" but, instead, many good—although not perfect—resources, all easily accessible through contemporary technologies. Most of all, resources, lessons, and videos *designed to promote further reflection, refinement, and inquiry—not for imitation and replication.*

PORTRAIT #4: Virtual Treasure Chest

The image of a treasure chest signifies the collection and preservation of hard-won assets. When something is of value, enthusiasts who recognize its worth, seek it out, study its history, and make it publicly available for others who will appreciate its unique origin, utility, and purpose. Without this intentional effort, valuable treasures are sometimes lost, forgotten, or simply overlooked. Others remain hidden in obscure locations that will likely take decades to rediscover.

In the education profession, knowledge of teaching practice is one such precious asset. Few things are more rewarding in the career of a teacher, or a community of teachers, than those moments of breakthrough and insight when a skillfully executed instructional practice leads to a successful student outcome.

These pivotal moments of discovery and advancement are what ignite and sustain the passion for teaching: figuring out and sharing solutions to persistent learning problems, adding a new asset to the treasure chest of knowledge and insights, and expanding one's repertoire of nuanced instructional practices that gradually accumulate over the course of a career.

Unfortunately, in most cases, these valuable assets of teacher knowledge are neither systematically pursued nor carefully preserved. Late in his career, Dewey (1929) noted that one of the saddest things about American education is that "the successes of [good teachers] tend to be born and die with them.... No one can measure the waste and loss that have come from the fact that the contributions of such men and women in the past have been thus confined" (p.10).

The word *virtual* is a key adjective for this metaphor. Rather than a static, traditional image of a pirate's chest where collectibles are locked up and hidden from view, this virtual treasure chest enables an active exchange of knowledge and insights through web-based, digital technologies (see circuit board in the foreground of the portrait). As the following examples illustrate, it provides a dynamic access point to preserve and retrieve these hard-won assets, so they might benefit next year's learners, so they might stimulate inquiry for other practitioners, and so they might be refined and adapted for learners in other contexts.

Accessing Digital Libraries: Elementary Math Example

One helpful example of a virtual treasure chest, developed by the Mills College Lesson Study Group (n.d.), can be found at http://lessonresearch.net/ttp/ (see Figure 4.1). Generated through expert facilitation of lesson study, this site provides a rich set of digital resources from a network of elementary school practitioners working on fractions and areas of polygons while using an approach called teaching through problem-solving (TTP). The project was designed to support lesson study and collaborative inquiry projects for U.S. teachers adopting the Common Core State Standards.

Available resources from the TTP site include detailed notes outlining both teacher and student experiences across each TTP lesson phase; complete unit plans, lesson plans and videos for each mathematical topic and grade level (K–4); content knowledge resources for each topic including full analyses of anticipated student thinking; pictures and diagrams of *bansho* (board writing) and corresponding work samples from student journals; specific notes for teacher questioning during each phase of the TTP lessons; guidance for engaging students in *neriage* (polishing ideas through

■ **Figure 4.1: Teaching Through Problem-Solving (TTP) Digital Library.** *Used with permission from Mills College Lesson Study Group*

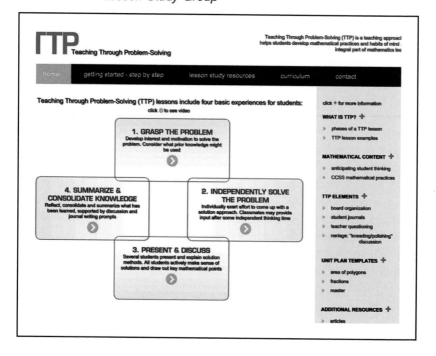

discussion); unit plan templates, links, and resources for conducting lesson study; and research articles for additional reading.

Project leaders indicate these materials have helped support high-quality lesson study cycles by providing video examples and other important resources to deepen lesson planning (C. Lewis, personal communication, December 5, 2014). A randomized control study with the fractions portion of the materials also showed significant impact on both students' and teachers' mathematical knowledge (Lewis, Perry, Friedkin, & Roth, 2012; Perry & Lewis, 2011).

Accessing Digital Libraries: Secondary Math Example

A second example of a virtual treasure chest comes from the TIMSS video website (http://timssvideo.com), a digital library with 53 representative lesson videos from seven countries, complete with lessons plans, lesson resources, expert commentary, and full lesson transcripts (see Figure 4.2).

■ **Figure 4.2: TIMSS Video Digital Library.** *Used with permission from the University of California, Los Angeles*

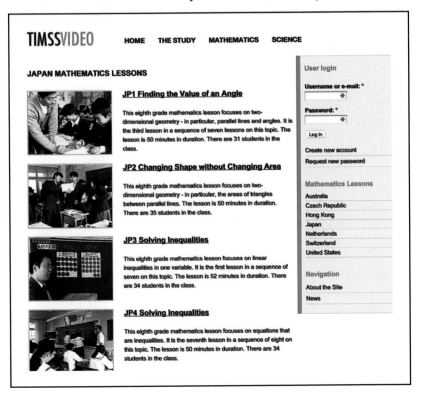

The site is designed for both practitioners and researchers to explore and investigate math and science teaching practices from other countries.

In the sections that follow, we use a Japanese math video from this TIMSS site to provide a more extended description of how digital libraries might be used to deepen professional knowledge of collaborative teacher teams. The story demonstrates how the Japanese video and corresponding digital resources helped a U.S. high school math team move beyond procedural teaching to adopt a more conceptual instructional approach.

Exploring a Japanese Math Video. Watch one of the Japan videos from the TIMSS library—more specifically, Mathematics Video 3 on solving inequalities—and you'll see that after giving his students a challenging problem to solve, the eighth grade math teacher strolls among the students' desks for almost 15 minutes, leaning over to see what each student is doing, making brief comments to each one, and noting on a chart how different students are solving the problem. Some are counting, some are making tables or charts, and some are writing equations. You will also notice the teacher does not provide students with any specific procedure or instructions for solving the problem either before assigning them to groups or as he circulates around the class.

The teacher clarifies instructions for one student: "Yes, write your explanation on the paper next to the problem." He clarifies terms for another: "This $180 - 10x$ you wrote—whose money is this?" He nudges others forward: "So you counted all the way? Is there an easier method to find the answer?" And he supports and acknowledges more complex approaches: "If you try combining this and that, you can make a mathematical expression." "So you wrote a simultaneous equation—OK!"

At the end of the lesson, the teacher strategically calls up several students to present their problem approaches to the class and then uses these examples to help students think critically about the different approaches they can use to solve similar problems.

As we described in Chapter 2, this process of roving among desks to monitor and assist students' independent or collaborative work is known as *kikan shidō*, a technical term used by Japanese educators to describe "between-desks instruction." In his commentary, which is linked to the solving inequalities lesson, a national research coordinator points out specific video segments where the Japanese teacher used *kikan shidō* to engage and support students' independent work.

The teacher purposely speaks loudly when giving advice to a student so that other students can hear. . . . The teacher could exploit the advantages of a whole-class instruction method . . . by doing *kikan shidō.* The teacher instructs students while strolling among the students' desks, thinking about the upcoming order of presentations for successful whole-class instruction. . . . The teacher carries a lesson plan sheet and writes down the students' understandings of—or difficulties with—a solution, while instructing individual students. (UCLA & the Carnegie Foundation for the Advancement of Teaching, n.d., 05:10)

Sharing the Japan Video With U.S. Teachers. While supporting math teachers involved in collaborative inquiry teams, we have often used this TIMSS video (and accompanying resources) to stimulate discussion of what a conceptual math lesson might look like. In fact, as part of a pilot project in the same district as the award-winning middle school described earlier, we shared this video with a group of high school algebra teachers.

After studying the video together and discussing the process the Japanese teacher used, the high school team prepared and implemented similar lessons in each of their classes that placed students in small groups to solve a challenging, multistep problem using systems of linear equations. The problem read as follows:

Your friend has interviewed for two different sales positions in competing companies. The Stellar Company pays $500 per week plus 10 percent commission on the total dollars from sales per week. The Lunar Company pays $200 per week but offers a 20 percent commission on the total dollars from sales per week. Sales at both companies are seasonal. Your friend wants some help determining which job option is best.

After carefully introducing the problem and placing students in groups, the teachers circulated around the room, recorded the approach that each group selected to solve the problem (table, graph, or system of equations), and asked questions to elicit and understand students' thinking. For students who were using a table to solve the problem, the teachers anticipated that they might struggle to find how the total amount earned would change for each job. They asked questions such as these: "How are the variables changing?" "How fast are the two jobs moving together?" For students who selected a graph, the teachers wanted to see whether they understood the solution conceptually. They asked those students questions like, "What data do you have?" "What are you going to put on each axis?" and "What is the graph going to tell you?" For students using the system of linear equations to solve the problem algebraically, teachers paid close attention to how they set up the problem. Teachers asked, "What variables did you choose, and what does each represent?"

Each method the students chose revealed underlying patterns of reasoning. Students who chose a table to solve the problem were typically less comfortable determining appropriate scale and intervals for a graph. They were also less likely to recognize when a problem involved a system of equations. The table represented a concrete and trusted format for organizing data, calculating values, and thinking through the solution.

Students who chose to solve the problem graphically typically recognized the need for two linear equations and saw the graph as a useful way to identify the point of intersection. They felt confident working with a more abstract representation and less computation.

Students who chose to solve the problem algebraically were comfortable visualizing the problem without all the detailed computation or graphical representation. They viewed the system of equations as the quickest, most reliable method and perhaps recognized that graphing could be imprecise when plotting values that involve decimals.

In the course of their observations, the teachers identified several groups to present their solutions at the end of the period. They ensured that each of the three main approaches—table, graph, and system of equations—was represented.

Much like the Japanese TIMSS video the teachers studied, the goal of this lesson was to help students better understand the continuum of problem-solving approaches, starting with more concrete methods (creating a table) and moving toward more sophisticated and abstract ones (using a system of equations). By strategically selecting students to present each method, the teachers highlighted the validity and benefits of all three methods but also pointed out the value and necessity of the algebraic approach for tackling mathematical problems with increased scale and complexity.

This example from TIMSS and a U.S. high school team demonstrates the potential of digital libraries to connect teachers engaged in inquiry with rich examples and alternative approaches from classroom contexts in other school communities—locally, nationally, or even around the

world. Much like other teachers we
observed in this same school district,
the algebra teachers had traditionally approached similar lessons by
first introducing procedures and
then using the *challenge problem* or
concept task as a culminating activity to evaluate student proficiency.
However, given timely access to
resources that were directly related

**Other Example
Digital Libraries**

- Teaching and Learning
  Exploratory: https://tle.soe
  .umich.edu/
- Teaching Channel: https://www
  .teachingchannel.org/

to their curriculum and inquiry context, these teachers were able to set
aside traditional scripts for math teaching and investigate a method they
had never considered before. Like the science case study in Chapter 2,
implementation varied across teachers, but all group members made initial
attempts to adopt this more conceptual lesson approach.

Develop Professional Judgment

A virtual treasure chest of teaching assets, made possible by digital libraries, might help teacher teams push beyond what they already know. But
unless teachers develop the judgment to effectively implement each
resource, one additional problem remains. The problem arises not only
in planning what instruction will be most effective for our students, but
it also arises on-the-fly during the course of a lesson when, for example, student misunderstanding requires further explanation and targeted
reinstruction or when students ask for assistance during a challenging
problem or task.

Teacher professional judgment can have a significant effect on classroom
teaching and student learning, as some recent research has confirmed. A
series of innovative studies has shown that teachers better able to analyze lesson videos score higher on classroom teaching quality, and their
students do better on learning assessments. Kersting, Givvin, Sotelo, and
Stigler (2010) developed an online activity using video clips from mathematics lessons and asked eighth grade teachers to analyze teaching and
write comments on key elements of instruction, such as how to improve
instruction they observed in the lesson clips. Two findings are especially
relevant to this discussion.

First, teacher ability to analyze lesson clips correlated with a measure of
their knowledge of mathematics. Second, their suggestions for improvement were highly predictive of student learning gains. Students of teachers

who included more or better suggestions for improving teaching learned more from a fractions unit than did those taught by teachers who offered no or ineffectual improvement suggestions.

In a second study, Kersting et al. (2012) again asked teachers to view video clips from fraction lessons that were good but not superlative examples of instruction. This time they added another element—the researchers observed teachers teaching a lesson in their own classrooms. Observations of the quality of teacher's instructional practice in the classroom, how much they knew about mathematics, and their students' performance on a fractions test were predicted by how well that they could analyze clips of a lesson video taught by a stranger. Suggestions made for improved instruction was again one of the analytic categories that was predictive of student learning and, this time, with how well a teacher taught in the classroom.

Developing Judgment With Lesson Study Videos

Similar opportunities might be made available with lesson study by video recording research lessons and revisiting key segments to discuss instructional decisions, like the science teachers experienced in Chapter 3. While planning lab activities, the teachers identified pivotal episodes where students would struggle with scientific concepts. They anticipated misconceptions that would likely surface and brainstormed appropriate teacher responses that would help advance student thinking. Later, while studying video clips of these same "struggle episodes," we asked them to record misconceptions and teacher responses that materialized in the lesson. During face-to-face reflection meetings, we collectively discussed these decisions in relationship to the plans we outlined. For example, when students were struggling with the osmosis and diffusion discovery lab, Amy used the following questions to nudge forward a group's thinking: "Do you think the molarity of the bag might change as it's soaking in the sugar water?" or "Why are you measuring the cups?" Was this too much guidance? Not enough guidance? What other questions might have been effective at that moment in the lesson?

Developing Judgment Through Live Observations

Teacher teams might also study episodes of professional judgment during live observations by following the same process of lesson study planning and reflection. For example, while collectively observing the algebra lesson on the better-paying job (described in the previous section), teachers could distribute themselves around the room and divide up data collection responsibilities for specific groups of students. During key lesson episodes, they could specifically take notes on misconceptions that emerged and the teacher-student interactions that transpired. They could discuss these observations in the post-lesson reflection meetings just as the science teachers did with the videos. They could also discuss *kikan shidō* choices in the lesson, such as which groups were selected to present at the end of the period. Did these examples help facilitate a rich discussion on the range of problem approaches? Given the options available from the various approaches observed in data collection, what were some other possibilities, and how might they have added to or detracted from the culminating discussion?

Conclusion

These observations and studies suggest that both expanding knowledge and developing judgment to use it well are probably keys to better-quality teaching and student learning. These two functions—knowledge and judgment—are likely essential if we are to assist teacher teams to raise the bar on what they try to improve. Instead of imitating so-called best practices or relying on long-established cultural scripts, accessing instructive examples and resources from digital libraries and discussing ways to improve instruction could enhance local knowledge and inquiry efforts while also strengthening connections to the global teaching community.

But given how often teacher teams hit a ceiling effect on what they attempt to improve, what might prompt them to question assumptions, access outside resources, and explore alternative approaches as they engage in collaborative inquiry? What might help them identify blind spots in their practice and prompt them to consider what they don't know, like the external assistance provided to the high school math team in this chapter? What might help them deepen their understanding of the skills and mindsets for investigating practice, as described in Chapters 2 and 3? And what might help them remain focused on steady growth and incremental progress in the midst of external pressures and competing demands for time and attention, as described in Chapter 1? These important questions bring us to the focus of our next chapter—a reconceived model for school leadership, settings, and assistance.

REFLECTION QUESTIONS

KEY PRINCIPLE: *Hard-won assets of local knowledge should be diligently pursued, continually refined, and globally shared.*

1. This chapter describes three common problems with best practices. How prevalent are these problems in your school community? What are some specific examples? How might you shift your focus to studying effective practices related to specific learning goals?

2. What opportunities are available for your school community to seek out new knowledge and alternative approaches? What opportunities do you have for generating and contributing knowledge for other practitioners? How might you improve these opportunities?

3. How often do you observe lessons (live or video recorded) and reflect together on specific instructional decisions? What might you do to foster growth in this area?

4. Reflect on your practice. What are some areas where you might be overconfident in your level of knowledge? Where might you find resources to address these needs?

ADDITIONAL RESOURCES

- See Leader's Guide in the Appendix for additional team exercises from this chapter and presentation ideas for the "Virtual Treasure Chest" portrait.
- Visit the companion website to download presentation slides, including a full color digital image of the portrait. Also find customizable templates, checklists, and tools to assist your implementation efforts.

Available at http://www.corwin.com/ErmelingTeachingBetter

REFERENCES

Clark, C. M., & Bjork, R. A. (2014). When and why introducing difficulties and errors can enhance instruction. In V. A. Benassi, C. E. Overson, & C. M. Hakala (Eds.), *Applying the science of learning in education: Infusing psychological science into the curriculum* (pp. 20–30). Society for the Teaching of Psychology. Retrieved from http://teachpsych.org/ebooks/asle2014/index.php

Cochran-Smith, M., & Lytle, S. (1999). Relationships of knowledge and practice: Teacher learning in communities. *Review of Research in Education, 24,* 249–305.

Dewey, J. (1929). *The sources of a science of education.* New York, NY: Horace Liveright.

Gallimore, R. (1996). Classrooms are just another cultural activity. In D. L. Speece & B. K. Keogh (Eds.), R*esearch on classroom ecologies: Implications for inclusion of children with learning disabilities* (pp. 229–250). Mahwah, NJ: Erlbaum.

Graff-Ermeling, G. (2007). *Building coherence: The role of an externally supported, site-based leadership team, in sustaining settings for instructional improvement.* Santa Monica, CA: LessonLab Research Institute.

Hiebert, J., Gallimore, R., Garnier, H., Givvin, K. B., Hollingsworth, H., Jacobs, J., . . . Stigler, J. (2003). *Teaching mathematics in seven countries: Results from the TIMSS 1999 video study* (NCES 2003–013). Washington, DC: US Department of Education, National Center for Education Statistics.

Hiebert, J., Gallimore, R., & Stigler, J. W. (2002). A knowledge base for the teaching profession: What would it look like and how can we get one? *Educational Researcher, 31*(5), 3–15.

Hiebert, J., & Grouws, D. A. (2007). The effects of classroom mathematics teaching on students' learning. In F. K. Lester (Ed.), *Second handbook of research on mathematics teaching and learning* (pp. 371–404). Charlotte, NC: Information Age.

Hiebert, J., Stigler, J. W., Jacobs, J. K., Givvin, K. B., Garnier, H., Smith, M., . . . Gallimore, R. (2005). Mathematics teaching in the United States today (and tomorrow): Results from the TIMSS 1999 video study. *Educational Evaluation and Policy Analysis, 27,* 111–132.

Kersting, N. B., Givvin, K., Sotelo, F., & Stigler, J. W. (2010). Teacher's analysis of classroom video predicts student learning of mathematics: Further explorations of a novel measure of teacher knowledge. *Journal of Teacher Education, 61,* 172–181.

Kersting, N. B., Givvin, K. B., Thompson, B. J., Santagata, R., & Stigler, J. W. (2012). Measuring usable knowledge: Teachers' analyses of mathematics classroom videos predict teaching quality and student learning. *American Educational Research Journal, 49*(3), 568–589.

Lewis, C., Perry, R., Friedkin, S., & Roth, J. (2012, November/December). Improving teaching does improve teachers: Evidence from lesson study. *Journal of Teacher Education, 63,* 368–375.

Little, J. W. (2003). Inside teacher community: Representations of classroom practice. *Teachers College Record, 105*(6), 913–945.

Mills College Lesson Study Group. (n.d.). *Teaching through problem-solving.* Retrieved from http://lessonresearch.net/ttp/index.html

Perry, R., & Lewis, C. (2011). *Improving the mathematical content base of lesson study: Summary of results.* Mills College Lesson Study Group. Retrieved from http://www.lessonresearch.net/IESAbstract10.pdf

Shulman, L. S. (1986). Those who understand: Knowledge growth in teaching. *Educational Researcher, 15*(2), 4–14.

Stigler, J., & Hiebert, J. (1999). *The teaching gap: Best ideas from the world's teachers for improving education in the classroom.* New York, NY: Free Press.

Thompson, B., & Stigler, J. (2008). *Final report of math research and development project at school X.* Santa Monica, CA: LessonLab Research Institute.

UCLA & the Carnegie Foundation for the Advancement of Teaching. (n.d.). NRC commentary on JP3 inequalities. *TIMSS Video.* Retrieved from www.timssvideo.com/49

This chapter was adapted from previously published work in the following:

Ermeling, B. A., & Graff-Ermeling, G. (2014, October). Teaching between desks. *Educational Leadership, 72*(2), 55–60. Alexandria, VA: ASCD. ©2014 by ASCD. Adapted with permission. Learn more at http://www.ascd.org

Ermeling, B. A., Hiebert, J., & Gallimore, R. (2015, May). Best practice: The enemy of better teaching. *Educational Leadership, 72*(8), 48–53. Alexandria, VA: ASCD. ©2015 by ASCD. Adapted with permission. Learn more at http://www.ascd.org

Gallimore, R., & Ermeling, B. A. (2012). Why durable teaching changes are elusive, and what might we do about it? *The Journal of Reading Recovery, 12*(1), 41–53. Adapted with permission from *The Journal of Reading Recovery,* http://www.readingrecovery.org. All rights reserved.

Matching Vision With Resources

A Reconceived Model for Leadership and Assistance

Winter Horseshoes

KEY PRINCIPLE

Investments in bold ideas should be matched by an equal investment in support and attention to detail.

PORTRAIT #5: Winter Horseshoes

During an 1812 military campaign, Napoleon made an ambitious decision to invade Russia. He launched his invasion in June with hopes of a relatively quick campaign that would finish before the winter months. Driven by an impressive record of recent conquests, Napoleon was operating with a spirit of invincibility and bold confidence in his strategy.

Saul David (2012), professor of war studies at the University of Buckingham, explains the enormous size and ambitious timeline of Napoleon's campaign:

> This was a logistical operation of quite staggering proportions, requiring a wagon train of no fewer than 26 battalions—eight equipped with 600 light and medium wagons each, and the rest with 252 four-horse wagons capable of carrying 1.36 tons (a grand total of 9,300 wagons).
>
> To pull these wagons and to transport his cavalry and artillery he had gathered 250,000 horses, all of which required 9kg (20 lbs.) of forage a day.
>
> And yet the figures did not add up.
>
> Had Napoleon arrived in Moscow in two months, and with only half his original 400,000 men, he would still have required total supplies of 16,330 tons, which was almost double the capacity of his supply trains. (paras. 7–10)

As the winter months drew near and his large army was traveling across difficult terrain, all of Napoleon's hopes and aspirations for victory were forfeited largely because of a few simple logistical oversights and miscalculations that exacted an overwhelming toll on his army. One of these oversights was failing to plan for the possibility of an extended campaign and the corresponding need for winter horseshoes.

Rather than meeting Napoleon in battle, the Russian army chose to withdraw, prolonging the conflict well into the fall and winter. While chasing the Russians through dense forests and marshes, Napoleon suffered great losses to his army and was finally forced to retreat just as the brutal winter months ensued.

David (2012) explains that this was only the beginning of Napoleon's problems:

Having entered Russia in June, and anticipating a short campaign, his horses were still shod with summer shoes. . . . This tiny logistical oversight was to cost him dear. Winter horseshoes are equipped with little spikes that give a horse traction on snow and ice, and prevent it from slipping. Without them, a horse can neither tow a wagon uphill, nor use them as brakes on the way down. (paras. 16–18)

Unable to traverse up and down hills, the horses were devastated with broken legs and other immobilizing injuries, which left the Grandee army without supplies. The troops began to waste away from starvation, and Napoleon's bold campaign ended in a tragic defeat.

The winter horseshoes provide an important reminder that while investing in bold strategies and ideas, leaders must also invest in adequate support and attention to detail. It's common for leaders to say, "I'm an ideas person, not a details person" as if to justify a one-dimensional approach to leadership. Whether it comes naturally or not, leadership, by necessity, involves both ideas and details, both vision and execution, both high expectations and support for accomplishing goals. So much of assisting others to follow through and execute a bold strategy comes down to attending to these details, which may go unnoticed when handled well, but threaten to derail the whole enterprise if and when neglected.

Traditional Patterns of Assistance

For school leaders, the lesson of the "winter horseshoes" means thinking through the details, resources, time, and assistance required to help teachers sustain the pursuit of teaching better and advance to new levels of knowledge. This is especially challenging when working to support school-wide implementation with multiple teacher teams. Checking in with teacher leaders; keeping track of each group's progress; and assisting teams to study, plan, and reflect on instruction in ways that stimulate growth in teaching and learning are all tasks that demand significant time and effort. But it's attention to these details that often defines the success or failure of an improvement "campaign." Our observations and experience suggest that most school leaders respond to this challenge with one of the following three approaches:

- Focus on the fires: One approach many leaders take, either by choice or by perceived necessity, is to devote all of their assistance to the most problematic groups—those that have less capable teacher leaders, weak content knowledge, or dysfunctional group dynamics.

- Manage every meeting: Other leaders set out to accomplish the impossible, attempting to be directly present in every meeting and managing or directing the work of each team.
- Back off and buffer: Yet another response by some leaders is simply to back off and serve as a buffer to protect teachers from distractions. These leaders indicate that it's impossible to manage or assist every team, so they limit their role to securing and protecting time with no attempt to engage in direct assistance or support.

Each of these approaches is based on a clear rationale, but each also presents some clear limitations for assisting teams and team leaders to get lasting results with collaborative inquiry. Much like a classroom, focusing only on problem groups prevents other teacher teams from receiving valuable feedback and assistance. It also disproportionately shapes the leader's perspective of work in the building by restricting opportunities for contact with other more productive teams. On the other hand, the leader who tries to "do it all" and directly manage every team inevitably runs out of steam and also runs the risk of micromanaging team leaders who need a balance of support and autonomy. By further contrast, the leader who backs off and chooses simply to buffer teachers from distractions leaves teams and leaders without critical assistance and risks being perceived as disinterested or devaluing teachers' collaborative work.

Strategically Assisting Performance

The artful task of leadership requires a delicate balancing act that incorporates elements of each of these approaches: securing and protecting time, identifying capable leaders, and distributing assistance efficiently and effectively across multiple teams. This represents a shift in emphasis from management and control to strategically assisting performance (Tharp & Gallimore, 1988). Elmore (2000) describes it as the reciprocity of accountability and capacity. "If the formal authority of my role requires that I hold you accountable for some action or outcome, then I have an equal and complementary responsibility to assure that you have the capacity to do what I am asking you to do" (p. 19). Supporting collaborative teams and team leaders so that each group responsible for improving outcomes has a direct line of assistance and feedback is one such responsibility.

This makes sense in principle, but practically speaking, how does a school leader make this happen? There is no single answer to this challenge, but with careful planning and thoughtful execution there are several key practices that can help leaders coordinate and sustain effective assistance.

Establishing a Triadic Model of Settings and Assistance

The first key practice is establishing an underlying system or infrastructure of settings and assistance that serves as the central mechanism for coordinating other key practices and strategies. We will refer to this system as the *Triadic Model* (Tharp & Gallimore, 1988; Tharp & Wetzel, 1969).

The idea behind the Triadic Model is to help schools solidify a regular pattern of settings and assistance routines dedicated to improving teaching and learning. This includes not only teachers but all educators in the school responsible for supporting teacher teams and overseeing instructional programs. As noted in Chapter 3, a setting is defined as "any instance in which two or more people come together . . . over a sustained period of time in order to achieve certain goals" (Sarason, 1972, p.1). Each role group needs a setting for learning where the members focus on improving their assistance, leadership, and teaching for the next immediate role group they support. While not every role group has the direct responsibility of teaching students, each does represent an important link in the chain of assistance, which significantly contributes to the work of the classroom.

Figure 5.1 shows the most basic assistance relationship in the Triadic Model. A represents teachers; B represents students. The line between A and B represents a *proximal line of assistance*—an individual (in this case a teacher) assisting the learning of the next immediate role group (the students).

■ **Figure 5.1: Proximal Line of Assistance for Students**

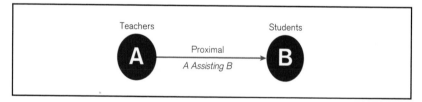

In Figure 5.2, we view the lines of assistance through the lens of a school leader, represented by A, and the roles of teacher and student are now labeled B and C. The line between B and C is still a proximal line of assistance—the teacher (B) directly assisting the learning of students (C). The line between A and B is also a proximal line of assistance—the school leader (A) directly assisting teacher learning (B). A more accurate way to describe this, however, is that A is assisting B's learning of how to assist C. In other words, the leader is assisting the teacher's learning of how to assist student learning.

■ **Figure 5.2: Proximal Lines of Assistance for Teachers and Students**

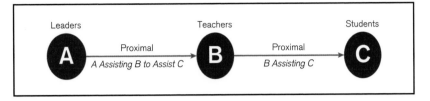

In Figure 5.3, the line between A and C (leader and student) represents a *distal line of assistance*—an individual (in this case a school leader) attempting to assist learning of an individual or role group that is one or more layers removed.

■ **Figure 5.3: Distal Line of Assistance for Students**

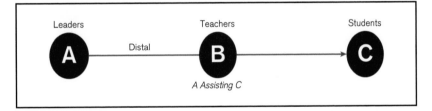

These simple diagrams provide an important schema or framework by which to conceptualize a school leader's role in the change process of an organization. The central premise of the Triadic Model is that the best way to influence learning in a distal setting is to focus on the support provided for learning in the proximal settings. Too often, school leaders focus the majority of their time and attention on how to create productive learning settings and routines for the distal setting (students) but neglect to invest an equal amount of time in creating the conditions for learning in their most proximal settings (teachers).

As we unpack this a bit further, the model can be expanded to encompass additional layers and tailored for use with any school initiative. Figure 5.4 represents a Triadic Model of settings and assistance specifically designed to support collaborative instructional inquiry or lesson study. At the apex of the triangle, teacher teams (C) meet three to four times per month to cycle through the inquiry process and study their practice as they work to assist the learning of students in the classroom (D). As a general rule,

■ **Figure 5.4: Triadic Model of Assistance for Collaborative Inquiry**

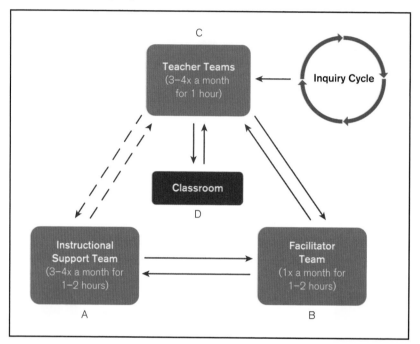

these teams should be no smaller than three teachers and no larger than seven teachers to maximize participation and contributions from each individual member.

Each teacher team should have an identified teacher facilitator who is trained and supported to lead collaborative work during these meetings. These facilitators, one representing every group in the school, also have a dedicated setting for learning where they come together as a facilitator team. The facilitator team (B) meets monthly to think through, study, and prepare for leadership of the teacher teams (C) with the goal of becoming increasingly effective in assisting teachers' learning of how to assist student learning (D).

The facilitator team receives leadership and assistance from the instructional support team (IST), which includes designated key administrators and other support staff. The IST (A) meets weekly to think through, study, and prepare for their leadership and support of the facilitator team (B) with the goal of becoming increasingly effective in assisting facilitators' learning of how to assist teachers' learning (C). While the facilitator team provides the primary assistance to the teacher teams, the IST also augments those efforts with strategic visits to selected teams at different points in the process. This is represented by the dotted line of proximal assistance between A and C.

Together these three role groups (A, B, C) function as part of a system of settings and assistance with each layer directly focused on support of the next role group. The bidirectional arrows illustrate the importance of incorporating feedback loops as part of this system. Providing assistance, like classroom teaching, is not a static process or simple delivery model. It's a dynamic, bidirectional process where each role group is listening, observing, and collecting feedback and evidence from their assistance efforts to guide and inform future action. This helps translate meetings into settings for learning and helps teams sustain improvement work over time, while many other priorities and tasks compete for time and attention. As described in the next sections, the Triadic Model of assistance also serves as a central mechanism for incorporating other key practices and capacity-building strategies that enable school leaders to organize settings, strategically distribute assistance, and help teams develop knowledge about teaching and learning.

Organizing Settings for Productive Work

One of the most overlooked "winter horseshoes" for any school improvement effort is the mundane task of organizing and aligning settings to ensure productive work. Anyone believing a school or district isn't already trying to make improvements has not likely visited many American schools. What is more typical are schools that have been flooded year after year with new solutions for improving student achievement. Old "new solutions" are seldom formally discarded; rather, they accumulate over time and create a crisis in "bandwidth."

What's critical for the IST in these circumstances is not only to establish buy-in for collaborative inquiry, but also to work with teams and team leaders to inventory and align settings for every task perceived as necessary and important. Table 5.1 provides an example "Organizing Settings Chart" from Central Elementary School (pseudonym). What follows is a description of how IST members can use the chart to organize and align settings with each grade-level or subject-area team.

Inventory Topics and Tasks

The first step is for an IST member and team leader to conduct a full inventory of tasks that occupy various settings and meeting times for the identified teacher team (Column 1) as well as the projected time required for each task (Column 2). Examples might include debriefing the week's events, tracking and addressing individual student concerns, sharing materials for upcoming lessons, announcing changes in policy, planning for field trips, reviewing district benchmark assessments, and so on.

■ **Table 5.1: Example "Organizing Settings Chart" From Central Elementary School–Fifth Grade**

Description of Work (what needs to get done)	Amount of Meeting Time Needed (amount of time and frequency)	Setting Where This Could Be Done (team meetings, faculty meetings, e-mail, conference periods, etc.)
Inquiry meetings	3–4 hours per month	Use weekly early release (3 times per month for 70 minutes).
Tracking and addressing individual student concerns	35 minutes per week	Use weekly early release (1 time per month—first half of meeting).
Sharing materials for upcoming lessons or activities	20 minutes per week	Use weekly early release (1 time per month—second half of meeting).
Announcements about school policy or procedures	Minimal	Move most of this to e-mail or handle during quarterly pupil-free days (faculty meetings).
Debriefing recent events	None	Move these conversations to lunch or other informal settings.
Updates on textbook orders and other materials	None	Conduct these updates and plans over e-mail.
Field trip plans	1 hour in November 2 hours in March	Specific teachers will plan over e-mail and meet during conference periods.
Review benchmark assessments	90 minutes each quarter	Meet 10:30–12:00 on quarterly pupil-free days (faculty meetings).
Lunch supervisions assignments	None	Move this to e-mail.
Other unexpected items and business	15 minutes per week (as needed)	Use weekly early release (1 time per month—last 15 min. of meeting).

This is all the ordinary business of teacher teams, which—when left unaddressed—quickly replaces inquiry and overtakes meeting agendas. Some of it can be handled more efficiently through e-mail, some of it is mission critical and needs be intentionally scheduled, some of it could be delegated to individuals, some of it may not be necessary at all . . . *but* all of it is *perceived* as absolutely essential to existing work and school routines. From the teachers' perspective, even for those who are excited about the potential of collaborative inquiry, these items must be carefully inventoried and addressed for teams to feel comfortable focusing on instructional improvement.

Align Tasks and Settings

Once this inventory is complete, the IST member and team leader make a corresponding list of settings and communication opportunities where these tasks might be accomplished (common planning time, early release days, faculty meetings, lunch periods, weekly e-mails from the principal, pupil-free days, individual prep periods, etc.). By comparing and analyzing the lists, they work through the alignment of settings and tasks. First, they set aside the necessary time and settings for collaborative inquiry (ideally three to four hours per month). These settings are marked off as an unavailable for other business. Next, they identify items that can be handled through other communication channels (e.g., the principal agrees to send out a weekly e-mail with announcements and updates rather than funneling this information verbally through the team leader). They also identify items that can be delegated and completed by individuals, such as field trip planning or lunch supervision assignments. Finally, they work to align settings with the right kind of work—matching duration, frequency, and number of people with the type of work that needs to be done.

The IST member and team leader continue to work through the list, arriving at a set of important items that need to take place during face-to-face meeting times. After adding up the time required and aligning settings for these remaining tasks, they draft a calendar not only for the collaborative inquiry work, but also for the other important business they will be focusing on at different points throughout the year. They review this list for feedback and refinement with team members and then publish a final calendar. The IST repeats this process with each teacher team, grade level, or department. Throughout the year, IST members also support team leaders to publish agendas two or three days prior to meetings, helping groups stay equally organized for other items of business as well as time devoted to collaborative inquiry.

See the companion website for a customizable "Organizing Settings Template" (http://www.corwin.com/ErmelingTeachingBetter).

School leaders who have followed this strategy report unsolicited words of appreciation from their staff. Teachers report a sense of coherence and clarity about settings, the purpose of settings, and continuity across the year. The result is not only a stable, physical space and time to focus on instructional improvement but a stable, emotional and psychological space to make that work productive and meaningful.

Strategically Supporting Teams With an Assistance Matrix

Another key practice school leaders can adopt is the use of an Assistance Matrix. Simply stated, the Assistance Matrix is a planning tool IST members can use, within the framework of the Triadic Model and regular IST meetings, to prepare for ongoing strategic assistance to multiple teams and team leaders. The underlying premise of the matrix is to leverage the full range of existing contact points in a school community and translate them into opportunities for intentional assistance. This is accomplished by aligning the scope and type of support required for a particular team or team leader with the setting or contact point that best accommodates that assistance strategy. Using this approach, even the most informal interactions in the faculty lounge or hallway can become a vehicle for teaching and learning if thoughtfully prepared and implemented. This frees up time to focus on those groups or leaders who might need more extensive assistance during a particular week or month. By monitoring and updating the matrix regularly, all teams receive different levels of support during different weeks or months based on their fluctuating needs across the year. Table 5.2 provides an example Assistance Matrix for Central High School's (pseudonym) inquiry teams. What follows is a description of how the matrix is used in both elementary and secondary schools.

Customize Settings and Contact Points

The process begins by personalizing the matrix for a specific school, department, or other context where IST members are responsible for supporting multiple teacher teams. For the row headings on the far left side of the table, the IST makes a list of each participating teacher team. For the column headings across the top, the IST takes an inventory of all the potential settings or contact points that might be leveraged as opportunities for assistance. The example categories in Table 5.2 are a good place to begin, but schools may have additional contact points unique to their local contexts and routines.

■ Table 5.2: Example "Assistance Matrix" From Central High School

Central High School Assistance Matrix					Week of November 2, 2015	
Settings for Assistance →	Hallway Comment	E-Mail Exchange	Stop by Classroom	Schedule a meeting	Visit Team Next Week	Other
Algebra I & Geometry	T: Graphing approach looks promising.					T: Needs new cable for LCD projector.
Algebra II & Precalculus		T: Remind Sal to stop by Steve's room before implementation this week.				
World Language	T: Using chart paper to list ideas and synthesize themes was an effective way to build consensus.					
Life Science			M: See if Tina is feeling ready for leading the debrief session. Offer help.			
Physical Science					M: Stop by during 2nd half of meeting—help with anticipating student responses.	

(Continued)

■ Table 5.2: (Continued)

Central High School Assistance Matrix					Week of November 2, 2015	
Settings for Assistance →	Hallway Comment	E-Mail Exchange	Stop by Classroom	Schedule a meeting	Visit Team Next Week	Other
English 1 & 2				M: Need help with clarifying evidence they will collect.		
English 3 & 4				P: Meet with Joni to work on asking more questions and giving people time to think.		
World History					P: Stop by during 1st half of the meeting to assist with strategies for English learners.	
U.S. History		P: Send Jose e-mail with some positive feedback on his efforts to lead the goal-setting discussion.		P: Meet next Mon. to discuss outside resources for primary source documents.		

Determine and Record
Strategic Assistance Plans for Each Team

The IST members devote a portion of their regular meeting agenda to the specific task of reviewing and updating the Assistance Matrix. This time can be scheduled on a monthly, biweekly, or weekly basis depending on the frequency of meetings for the groups receiving support. The IST reviews the latest status of collaborative work for each team and determines the specific type of assistance, feedback, intervention, or deepening of knowledge that might be required and the setting or contact point best suited for this assistance strategy. The information is recorded on the matrix in the appropriate cells with enough detail that it will serve as a productive reminder later in the week. Each member of the IST is given responsibility for several teams (ideally three but no more than four), and each entry is preceded by a first name or initial to signify the person responsible for that strategy.

Involve Teams and Team
Leaders in Identifying Assistance Needs

As IST members develop relationships with their assigned teams, they should carefully explain their roles to the teams and team leaders, emphasizing their commitment to serve as a resource for assistance and support. They should also encourage teams to identify specific areas where they would like guidance, feedback, or opportunities to deepen knowledge, perhaps making this a standing agenda item during regular facilitator team meetings. Establishing these mutual expectations and demonstrating a commitment to listening and learning about each team's needs will help teachers and team leaders begin to embrace and even seek out assistance. In the words of one school administrator who diligently implemented this approach, "My role has shifted to that of a support provider. As I visit groups, I am there to help them in the process and provide assistance when they get stuck, not to evaluate or judge them. This also allows me to help them learn from their successes and gains."

Review the Matrix Daily and Implement Assistance

Each member of the IST prints a copy of the matrix or uploads a copy to a mobile device for reference and review on a daily basis as they implement assistance strategies. When appropriate, some IST members may also choose to update the matrix with notes, keeping track of how the team or team leader responds to the strategic assistance.

See the companion website
for a customizable "Assistance
Matrix Template" and a link to
the web-based version in Google
Sheets (http://www.corwin.com/
ErmelingTeachingBetter).

Update the Matrix and Collaborate Asynchronously

Another productive method for updating the matrix is to store the document as a spreadsheet online in a web-based interface where members can asynchronously access, record, and update their strategic assistance plans. The matrix can be replicated with a new tab for each week or month of scheduled meetings and corresponding support.

Reflect on Outcomes and Identify Areas for Improving Assistance

Over the course of a year, IST members can use the assistance matrix to look back and trace the patterns of assistance they have provided to teachers and reflect on the corresponding results of this support. Which groups or leaders seemed to experience the most growth and improvement? What aspects of assistance contributed to this progress? What groups were less productive? How might an assistance strategy be adjusted in the future to increase the likelihood of success?

This reflection process will also reveal growth opportunities for school leaders as they identify their own strengths and needs in providing assistance and communicating with teams. One improvement theme an IST might focus on is learning to provide clear, instructive feedback that includes useful information rather than vague statements of evaluation. For example, after observing a team meeting where the facilitator did an exceptional job of building consensus, the administrator might comment, "Using chart paper to list ideas, underline, and synthesize emerging themes was an effective way to build consensus" as opposed to a more general comment such as, "Good job in the meeting today." Other important skills to target for improvement might be learning to ask more questions before offering advice, or developing the discernment of when to intervene and when to let groups learn from their own experiences. After setting and sharing improvement goals like these examples, the IST can begin to brainstorm strategies for assisting various teams and even simulate scenarios for practicing and refining effective discourse and communication skills.

Coauthoring Inquiry Narratives

Finally, while providing this distributed assistance to assigned teams, one other effective practice for nurturing a relationship of support and reflective growth is for IST members to take on the role of coauthor in composing narrative summaries of a team's improvement journey. We refer to these narratives as *KTL Summaries* (**K**nowledge about **T**eaching and **L**earning).

What is a KTL Summary?

The KTL Summary is a concise narrative format that helps teams create meaning from their experiences—translating a sequence of complex developments from meetings and classroom interactions into tangible words and sentences that convey *tacit knowledge.* Tacit knowledge, by definition, refers to implicit ideas and expertise that practitioners accumulate about their craft that are idiosyncratic and hard to explain or replicate. Prior to being formally articulated, these implicit understandings contain gaps and holes that are typically overlooked and become obstacles to future application or transfer. Composing the KTL Summary helps uncover these gaps and compels teams to think more critically and elaborate more carefully about the nuances they discovered regarding the relationship between teaching and learning. So the term *knowledge,* in this case, does not imply conclusive evidence from formal science but rather emerging findings and insights from ongoing practitioner inquiry.

An effective KTL Summary addresses the following components and questions:

- What was the central problem or research theme the group felt compelled to address, and why was it compelling and important?
- What was the lesson context for the current cycle being reported?
- What was the team's working hypothesis? How was the instructional plan intended to address the problem and improve learning?
- What were the most pivotal instructional elements of the lesson?
- What did the evidence from the lesson suggest?
- What insights were gained about teaching and learning?
- What were the lingering questions or priorities for the next cycle of inquiry?

The coauthor role enables the IST member to develop a shared understanding of the story and participants, which cultivates mutual trust and opens the door for assistance, reflection, and learning. As opposed to monitoring teams for compliance or evaluation purposes, taking joint responsibility for chronicling reflective narratives establishes a nonthreatening purpose for asking questions and probing for details. The IST member can position these questions from the perspective of needing some help to better articulate the group's story.

What Does It Look Like in Action?

As an example, a principal was writing up the first draft of a KTL Summary for a high school English team that was working on the challenge of helping students use evidence to support assertions. After visiting a recent meeting where the team had examined evidence from a lesson implementation, the principal noticed some gaps in how the team articulated implications for future instruction. The teachers documented several important shortcomings in the way students were formulating arguments, but their primary instructional response to this problem was to come up with more creative activities for using evidence. The principal recognized they were likely missing something far more subtle and important. The teachers needed to explicitly model the sequence of reasoning required when identifying and explaining the connection between a selection of literary text and the thematic elements it supports. While updating the Assistance Matrix during an IST meeting, the principal decided to schedule some time with the facilitator during her conference period. He wanted feedback and input on the emerging draft of their KTL Summary as well as his observations about this potential missing element in their recent discussion.

As the facilitator read the summary and reflected on these questions, she began to notice the same gaps in the team's thinking and expressed a great sense of clarity and insight, which helped her redirect the team's approach for their next iteration of inquiry. Shortly after their conversation, the facilitator wrote the following message to her team in preparation for their upcoming meeting:

> Dear Team,
>
> Good morning, I hope all is well with you. This Tuesday is going to look a little different. We are going to pause for the first half of our time together to look at how we think. What we as a team are trying to do is get our students to make a huge jump between summary and synthesis, and the data we collected last time suggested the need for this skill more than ever. I think we need to spend a little time figuring out how we make that leap, so we can help our students do the same.
>
> After that, we will work on a hypothesis for our next lesson and hopefully begin planning with a brand-new arsenal of tools.
>
> I am looking forward to our time together, Tuesday at 7:15 a.m.

As illustrated with this example, the KTL Summary can be instrumental in creating a safe context for open discussion and reflection, disarming the typical barriers between teachers and school leaders and enabling participants to learn more about themselves and their work than would otherwise be possible. The reflective discussions can also be instrumental in expanding horizons of observation and "raising the ceiling" on a team's knowledge and improvement efforts.

What Are the Logistics?

Rather than waiting to compose summaries at the end of a project, IST members should construct drafts and request feedback from teams and facilitators incrementally as each stage of the process unfolds. This helps foster ongoing dialogue between IST members and facilitators and creates the opportunity for important midcourse corrections that can enhance the quality of the team's work. IST members should also include specific follow-up questions for facilitators as part of their regular updates to the Assistance Matrix and should incorporate the formal review of draft summaries as a consistent agenda item during monthly facilitator meetings.

The final product of an effective summary is a carefully crafted case description of teaching and learning conveying pivotal instructional insights and important findings that a team of teachers uncovered in their efforts to address an instructional problem. These findings can emerge from unsuccessful attempts and gaps teachers discover in their research lessons as well as successful approaches that yield positive learning results.

To maximize utility and accessibility, we suggest summaries be no longer than 1000 to 1500 words and should be written for an audience of teachers and educators. Summaries can be written as either first-person or third-person narratives. Using a blog site or other social media platform, teams can publish the summaries with short headlines and abstracts about their projects to increase visibility and opportunities for extended collaboration. Readers can scan a feeder page with multiple headlines to explore recently submitted summaries or search the archives for particular topics of interest.

Once completed, the summaries can be stored and retrieved as part of a digital library (see Chapter 4) along with the corresponding research lesson, accompanying materials, copies of student work, videos (if available), and other resources associated with the project. These resources can be attached to the summary through hyperlinks, so readers can drill down and explore more details.

We conclude this section with one complete example of a KTL Summary. The example was coauthored (in third person) by an IST member and a group of English teachers from Central High School. The length of the summary is 1120 words.

Example KTL Summary
Revisiting Revision (Central High School English Team)

Drawing on recent classroom assessments, the Central High School English Team (pseudonym) identified the following research theme: How do we help students *revise compositions with less attention to mechanics and greater emphasis on clarity of written arguments?* This was consistently a challenge for all teachers on the team and a critical aspect of their long-term goal for graduating students with strong writing skills.

Lesson Design and Rationale. For their first research lesson, they focused on a lesson in the English 1 curriculum just after students completed first drafts of a novel/movie comparison paper. The team developed several instructional approaches to tackle this challenge with revision, including a sequence of exercises where students were asked to study, rank, and justify the effectiveness of potential revisions to a writing sample. Teachers would then discuss potential revisions with the class, noting particularly strong student justifications and modeling, as needed, their own thinking and justifications for specific revisions. Teachers anticipated this might help students visualize the desired shift from mechanics to content. They also planned a group activity called *gossipy reading,* where they assigned students specific roles (reader, recorder, or commentator) to help students pause and think more carefully about revision work. The commentators were instructed to stop the group whenever they noticed specific errors with clarity or content.

Results From Observations. The evidence teachers collected from live observations revealed a majority of students genuinely grappling with ranking exercises and working to identify gaps in clarity and logic. What follows is a paragraph teachers used during the ranking exercise for revision commentary followed by four example revision comments they asked students to rank as a 0, 1, or 2.

> The obvious theme is women's struggle between domestic duties and personal growth. You see the stress in which the character of Jo March handles as she balances her work and family life. In the

novel, it is apparent that her family duties subtract from her ability to grow personally. The problem of being a seamstress, a teacher, and a caretaker creates conflict between *that* and being able to grow as a young woman into a young adult and live a carefree life finding herself.

A. The citations are missing.

B. The last sentence is too long.

C. Shouldn't say "you."

D. What problem? What is "that"?

During the discussion of this example, one student raised his hand and said, "Letter D is a 2." When asked to explain his answer, he replied, "You're leaving a cliff-hanger." Another student elaborated further, "You can't just say there is a problem and not explain it."

While teachers reported numerous observations of students successfully identifying similar gaps in analysis or reasoning, there was also evidence that students struggled to offer concrete suggestions for correcting these errors. During the modeling exercise for the group activity, one student commented, "The theme of the story is not explained clearly." When asked, "How would you move this from a Level 1 to a Level 2," he looked stumped and answered: "You state the theme more clearly."

Results From Student Work. The results from student work corroborated what teachers recorded in their observations. The papers demonstrated students had begun to make a significant shift in revision focus from superficial mechanics to writing content. The majority of case students were able to identify missing or insufficient conclusions, the lack of connections between ideas and the main point, and broad statements lacking specific detail. A smaller number of students, but more than anticipated, began to recognize instances where there was insufficient explanation of textual quotes incorporated as evidence. However, while error recognition improved, most students struggled to make suggestions for resolving identified writing problems.

Insights About Teaching and Learning. As the group reflected on the lesson and student work, their conversation focused on a pivotal discovery—the importance of teaching students what *clarity of analysis* and *revising for* *clarity of analysis* actually look like by providing examples of both and teaching students to rate the level of quality (0,1, or 2). This prepared students for monitoring their own revision work with the same mental framework and helped them move beyond superficial emphasis on punctuation and spelling. The teachers realized they had been telling students to focus on the clarity and effectiveness of their arguments but were not explicitly teaching students how to do that. During the post-lesson discussion, one teacher reflected:

> I was surprised by how engaged they were in the ranking task. Honestly, some of those kids . . . I didn't know they were capable of that focus because they are everywhere. . . . We touched on something that touched a chord and they understand. . . . And that was exciting for me because I knew it was what we were teaching. It was what we had created . . . .

The team agreed that the gossipy reading activity was a creative way to structure peer work, but without the modeling and ranking exercises, it would likely have limited impact. In addition to the importance of the modeling and ranking exercise, the teachers also discovered students performed better when taught to focus on one particular aspect of the paper at a time, focusing on connections between main idea and details, then focusing on textual quote explanations, and so on.

Looking Ahead. Energized by this new evidence of student progress, the team was eager to help students move beyond identification of errors and learn to make thoughtful corrections that enhance writing clarity. The teachers discussed how the modeling exercises had mostly focused on error recognition and instructive commentary that produced some positive results, but now they needed to model and teach methods for revising and correcting these common mistakes. One of their insights from observing the lesson was that teachers needed to elicit more thinking from students during discussion of sample papers. Rather than responding or elaborating on a student comment immediately, the team agreed it was important to ask more follow-up questions and extend class discussion. "How can we make this a level 2?" "What could you add to this sentence to strengthen the connection to the main point?" They also agreed it was important to introduce several concrete examples of how to improve writing in each of these critical areas. In particular, they needed to provide students with more examples of writing that does not "connect the dots" for the reader (e.g., textual quotes that are incorporated without sufficient explanation) and give students opportunities to experience the lack of clarity this creates from a reader's perspective. Finally, the team discussed how other courses should begin to incorporate this approach and explicitly teach levels of quality to help students with revision analysis.

Conclusion

Sustaining collaborative inquiry and improvement requires a dedicated effort across many months in the midst of myriad potential obstacles and distractions. This is possible only when both teachers and administrators are equally engaged and committed to the work. As one principal expressed:

> I've learned to apply what I'm learning to the structure of the whole school. Leaders at all levels of the school need to operate as "facilitators" rather than managers. This takes more work than just setting policy and delegating tasks. We have a feeling as a school that we're a community and everyone is learning. The role of the administrator is to be the primary model for this [assistance].

Teams that receive this kind of consistent support and feedback from their school leaders are far more likely to remain focused and productive. They are also more likely to question assumptions, consider alternatives, and broaden horizons, which in turn improves the quality of teaching and learning in the classroom.

By establishing a Triadic Model of settings and assistance, organizing and aligning settings, intentionally planning and differentiating assistance to each team, and coauthoring narratives that capture teachers' emerging insights, school leaders can foster a culture of support and encouragement that is highly valued by teachers, elevates the productivity of meetings, and nurtures an atmosphere of deeper learning for both students and adults. Taking a lesson from the winter horseshoes, they can also ensure that these bold and promising ideas are translated into practice rather than subjecting them to a tragic and premature demise through hasty implementation and inadequate support.

These strategies have proven effective in supporting and elevating the quality of collaborative work for a variety of team contexts. But even with dedicated assistance and support, some teams face unusually difficult circumstances with complex group dynamics, diverse curriculum assignments, or a history of unproductive meetings. These more challenging conditions can be discouraging and require even more strategic assistance and thoughtful support. In Chapter 6 we share two detailed examples and offer five specific suggestions to help school leaders refocus and revive problematic teams.

REFLECTION QUESTIONS

KEY PRINCIPLE: *Investments in bold ideas should be matched by an equal investment in support and attention to detail.*

1. The beginning of this chapter describes three traditional approaches school leaders use for supporting teacher teams (focus on the fires, manage every meeting, back off and buffer). How would you describe your current approach?

2. What aspects of the Triadic Model are in place at your school? What settings are missing? How could you make time for these settings? What leadership roles need to be created or changed to make this happen?

3. In what ways could you use the Assistance Matrix at your school? What steps could you take to begin implementing it?

4. If you play a role supporting collaborative inquiry, how well do you know your teams' stories? Think of a specific team. What assistance would you provide to help them close gaps in planning, knowledge, or judgment?

ADDITIONAL RESOURCES

- See Leader's Guide in the Appendix for additional team exercises from this chapter and presentation ideas for the "Winter Horseshoes" portrait.
- Visit the companion website to download presentation slides, including a full color digital image of the portrait. Also find customizable templates, checklists, and tools to assist your implementation efforts.

Available at http://www.corwin.com/ErmelingTeachingBetter

REFERENCES

David, S. (2012). Napoleon's failure: For the want of a winter horseshoe. *BBC News Magazine*. Retrieved from http://www.bbc.co.uk/news/magazine-16929522

Elmore, R. (2000). *Building a new structure for leadership*. Washington, DC: Albert Shanker Institute.

Sarason, S. (1972). *The creation of settings and the future societies*. San Francisco, CA: Jossey-Bass.

Tharp, R. G., & Gallimore, R. (1988). *Rousing minds to life: Teaching, learning, and schooling in social context*. Cambridge, England: Cambridge University Press.

Tharp, R. G., & Wetzel, R. J. (1969). *Behavior modification in the natural environment*. New York, NY: Academic Press, 1969.

This chapter was adapted from previously published work in the following:

Ermeling, B. A. (2012). Strategic opportunities: Matrix helps principals support multiple teacher teams. *The Learning Principal, 7*(2), 1, 4–7. Adapted with permission of Learning Forward, http://www.learningforward.org. All rights reserved.

CHAPTER 6

Multiplying Power

How Joint Productive Activity
Revived Two Problematic Teams

Joint Productive Activity (JPA)

KEY PRINCIPLE

Power is multiplied to the fullest extent when we work together productively.

B y now most schools or districts in the United States have participated in some form of teacher collaboration—learning communities, learning teams, inquiry teams, communities of practice, or even lesson study. While this is good news, our experience and observations suggest that what constitutes a learning community varies significantly in purpose and effectiveness across the United States.

For example, in at least a dozen districts we observed, the terms *learning community* or *teacher collaboration* were used to describe meetings where teachers were expected to work on mandated initiatives such as accreditation planning, district assessment analysis, or high-stakes test preparations. In other cases, schools had simply renamed as *learning communities* their faculty or department meetings covering textbooks, field trips, policy changes, or upcoming deadlines.

An even larger number of districts we visited had attended local or national workshops featuring compelling cases of high-performing schools that established exemplary learning communities. Energized by these ideas, school leaders developed new bell schedules, adjusted common planning times, and established new settings for collaboration. Unfortunately, what they lacked was enough detail on where to start the journey and how to keep moving forward. As a result, schools were left to devise their own implementation plans. One principal organized a book study on becoming a data-driven school, others tried to establish a tiered intervention system, some asked instructional coaches to provide professional learning, and others encouraged sharing and testing out "best practices" as teachers saw fit.

Sadly, in many of the contexts we've observed, settings like this have reduced collaboration to compliance-driven work, operational tasks, or loosely structured discussions rather than meaningful learning opportunities to study and improve teaching. This often leads to meetings characterized by complaints and frustration about wasted time and gives rise to other latent issues such as complex group dynamics and interpersonal conflict.

PORTRAIT #6: Joint Productive Activity (JPA)

In Japan, the word for *collaboration* (*kyōryoku*) consists of two Chinese characters, called *kanji* (see Figure 6.1). The character positioned at the top (協) is

■ Figure 6.1: Japanese for *Collaboration*

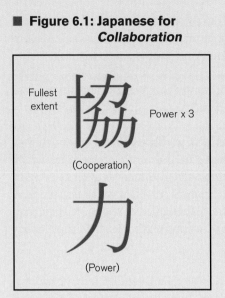

Fullest extent

Power x 3

(Cooperation)

(Power)

the symbol for cooperation, and the character positioned on the bottom (力) is the symbol for power. The cross-like symbol on the far left of the top character represents the number 10 or something being multiplied to the fullest extent. If you look closely at this top character, you also notice that it contains three smaller versions of *power*. So the word for *collaboration* in Japanese might be literally translated as, "power is multiplied to the fullest extent when we work together."

That's an insightful definition for collaboration, but it's important to add the implied meaning that "power is multiplied to the fullest extent when we work together . . . *productively.*" Every practitioner has suffered through an untold number of unproductive meetings, painfully reminding us that merely bringing people together is not sufficient to multiply the power. As illustrated by the boat passengers working together to navigate and harness the power of potentially destructive waves (see opening portrait), grouping people in teams can either greatly multiply or severely undermine instructional improvement efforts.

In Japan, collaboration is a way of life. Teachers do not schedule meetings simply for collaboration's sake. They routinely leverage the power of collaboration as a tool to set and share mutual goals, carefully develop instructional plans, test out practices in the classroom, and reflect critically on ways to improve.

The two stories in this chapter provide examples of U.S. teacher teams that overcame significant obstacles with complex group dynamics, diverse curriculum responsibilities, and a history of ineffective meetings. Both teams found new strength and unexpected reward from shifting the focus of meetings to JPA and systematic improvement of teaching.

Story #1: Focusing on Successful Action

The first JPA example comes from a large, urban middle school where the principal sought out Brad's guidance to revive their professional learning communities. They especially needed help with one teacher team whose meetings were suffocating from tension and hostility. When teachers on the team were asked to describe what happened during collaboration time, many responses included such confrontational behaviors as shouting, poor listening, hostility, negativity, and arguing about unimportant topics. Other teachers complained about a lack of relevance to daily teaching, wasted time, and reading uninformative books.

When Brad met with the team, he made two observations: "One, you don't like unproductive and contentious meetings, and two, you would like to have meetings that are productive and focused on improving teaching and learning. Does anyone disagree with that?"

The room was quiet. Their silent agreement defined a critical choice point. Some might have suggested team-building activities to exorcise the hostile social dynamics standing in the way of effective collaboration time—an approach that assumes attitudes must change before behavior changes. Brad assumed the opposite: behavior change is followed by attitude change.

Brad asked, "Can we all agree to suspend those behaviors that are disrupting productive work?" Heads nodded, and no one raised any opposition, so Brad continued, "Then let's get started by developing an agenda."

The team started searching for a shared problem they faced around teaching and learning, a pressing concern the group thought essential. Turning away from the highly abstract, philosophical questions that had led to so much conflict was what this group needed, not team-building activities.

Behavior change preceding attitude and belief changes is a staple narrative in literature, popular media, and personal anecdotes. Popular, sports-themed movies often share the same basic plot: a warring group of players rife with conflict gets a new coach who gradually knits together a team dedicated to a common goal. Players who did not like each other begin to work together through demanding effort and initial setbacks because each is in pursuit of the same outcome.

That is what happened with the middle school team.

The principal and Brad had regular calls in between each of his monthly visits. On those calls she would provide a synopsis of how things were going with each of her teacher teams and particularly this problematic group. She regularly attended their meetings to support the facilitator and tried to help moderate some of the contentious dialogue. She confided she had stopped trying to change their behavior through talk and recognized the futility of that approach.

Perhaps the most important thing the principal did was free up time in team meetings to focus on the new pattern of work they had initiated, which was identifying student instructional needs and working on plans for addressing them. She gave the teachers permission to discontinue some of the other less-defined activities, such as book studies and general discussions of students. These were leaving too much room for unproductive dialogue, debate, and conflict and were too far removed from teachers' daily classroom practice.

The principal worked hard to assist the team in following the same approach modeled during Brad's visits. Team members began to see this cycle of improvement as the new expectation for how they spent their meeting time, not just a short-lived experience for one or two meetings. The principal also made sure to celebrate the team's success in the larger school community, praising their efforts in staff meetings and highlighting positive results.

A few months after his initial visit, Brad returned for another series of meetings and discovered dramatic changes had taken place. Prior to arriving, the principal sent a short e-mail to share some encouraging signs of progress with the problematic group.

> I sat in on the team Wednesday and the meeting was great. . . . They had an agenda they stuck to. They looked at the pre-test they are going to administer in the reading classes this Friday, talked about the graphic organizer they are going to introduce next Monday in the social studies classes and reviewed some sample student work they had generated to see how the students

did prior to formal instruction. The time flew by and it was very interactive. If every day was like that—we would be way ahead of the game.

Following the pattern set in motion during the first visit, the principal and team facilitator made a weekly commitment to action-oriented agendas that continued to focus on planning, implementing, and reflecting on instruction related to student needs identified and shared by the group. The area they were focused on was reading comprehension, which they collectively defined as "the ability to connect what is being read with prior knowledge, ask relevant questions, and demonstrate understanding of ideas and information." The facilitator also sent a brief update a few days in advance of the next visit:

So we are currently working on a clear measurable objective [for reading comprehension]. The questions that have come up are very interesting.

What determines grade level?

What timeline should be used?

What is proficient?

What level of comprehension? Use of Bloom's taxonomy?

What strategies are used for reading comprehension?

I appreciate the more recently graduated teachers who are better in touch with the terminology. We are wondering if summarizing is the way to go. . . . We met twice this week, and the group seems excited and has contributed a great deal of input.

In the meeting Brad observed, the facilitator started the meeting on time, reviewed the agenda, and initiated a brainstorming process to identify promising instructional approaches for helping students with reading comprehension problems. A few times during the discussion, Brad observed a team member physically hold her hand over her mouth to suppress an impulsive response that previously might have derailed the meeting. By the end of the meeting, the team had outlined basic action steps for a lesson, and all members had contributed to the discussion and planning.

When the problematic team of teachers first began working on a shared problem, they did not like each other very much and shared no common instructional philosophy. But once they established a common goal for student learning and agreed on benchmarks for measuring success, a new pattern of successful interactions was set in motion, defined by a sense of shared purpose and urgency to improve student outcomes. The debating was over; the JPA had begun.

Story #2: Finding Common Ground

The second JPA example comes from a team of foreign language teachers at a large, suburban high school. The school had just initiated a weekly late start for students so that teachers could meet in collaborative teams instead of traditional department meetings. One foreign language group included three members who each taught the full range of courses, entry level through advanced, in their respective areas of language expertise. Cindy was responsible for German, Diane taught French, and Steven taught American Sign Language (teacher names are pseudonyms). Every Wednesday morning, teachers across the school met for 75 minutes to conduct inquiry around shared student learning needs. All other teachers in the foreign language department were members of the Spanish group, leaving this mixed group of singletons with the daunting challenge of forging a cohesive team. While they shared the experience of being foreign language instructors, their curriculums differed significantly with unique cultural and grammatical elements specific to their respective languages. Having dealt with these complexities in department meetings for many years, the team expressed skepticism about making collaboration work.

In addition to the challenge of diverse curriculum responsibilities, the group also faced a unique communication barrier. Steven was not only a sign language instructor but was also deaf with limited oral communication ability. He could communicate only through written English or sign language.

Cindy was the designated facilitator for the team and worked to engage Steven in the process by exchanging e-mails in advance regarding agendas and discussion topics. She used notepads and chart paper during meetings to facilitate dialogue and help Steven participate in group discussions. Cindy and Diane also learned to adapt their communication patterns to maximize Steven's participation—securing eye contact before speaking, mouthing words naturally without exaggerated lip movements, using shorter sentences as needed, and incorporating gestures or visual cues as much as possible.

Despite these commendable efforts, all three teachers grew weary of the communication obstacles after the first month and expressed frustration with how little they were able to accomplish during the weekly hour of meeting time. In one meeting, where they had planned 20 minutes of the agenda to brainstorm instructional strategies, they spent more than 45 minutes struggling to understand one of Steven's ideas through gestures and written dialogue. Steven began to feel self-conscious about slowing down the team's progress, and the other teachers felt uncertain about how to proceed.

The assistant principal and facilitator discussed the possibility of excusing Steven from meetings but first agreed to test out one more creative solution. Rather than meet face-to-face on Wednesday mornings, they gave Steven permission to remain at his house and dial-in for meetings by phone, using a government-sponsored video-relay service, which Steven had connected to his home television. Using this video-phone technology, Steven was able to communicate with a remote sign language translator who was also wearing a telephone headset and could directly connect by conference line with a third party of Steven's choice. So Cindy and Diane placed a speaker phone on the desk where Steven normally sat during their face-to-face meetings. Each Wednesday at 7:00 a.m. they received a call from a translator (a different person each week) who would play the part of Steven Anderson for the duration of the meeting. It was a bit strange adjusting to these different voices, both male and female, representing Steven without any direct face-to-face to contact, but the communication barrier was lifted. The group felt significant relief about the opportunity to engage in free-flowing dialogue and discussion.

While the pace of the meetings had picked up and the feasibility of group discourse had improved, the teachers still had to overcome a second challenge, which was navigating their diverse mix of languages and curriculums. As they inventoried typical student learning needs, the teachers focused primarily on challenges specific to the language they were teaching. In German, students commonly struggled with adjusting to three different genders and four different cases for nouns as well as proper use of articles der, die, and das. In French, students struggled with learning to pronounce words with accents, using contractions, and translating the verb to be. In American Sign Language, students needed to learn not only signs but also the position, direction, and distance for various hand movements.

This initial discussion was more of a debate about which language was most difficult to learn rather than a process of setting and sharing goals around common learning needs. But with guidance from the instructional support staff, the group continued to unpack their daily teaching goals and experiences and began to coalesce around one clear commonality. They were all working toward exclusive use of the target language (TL) in their daily instruction and trying to foster a classroom environment where students would gradually overcome anxieties about using the TL.

The teachers agreed that making the classroom as much like a second language context as possible was important for increasing exposure to the TL, particularly since class time represented the only opportunity most students would have to practice use of the language. They believed using the TL would help students view the language as more than a subject of study and begin to see value and purpose in the language even for ordinary things like understanding classroom terminology, routines, and instructions.

For Steven, relying exclusively on use of the TL was his only option. He spent his teaching career honing techniques and structuring his classroom routines to facilitate the use of sign language for all teacher and student interactions. His experience in this area unlocked a rich discussion and collaborative exchange where Diane and Cindy could glean insights from Steven and where Steven, in turn, could refine his understanding of various techniques by explaining them to his colleagues.

Building on these ideas from Steven, as well as other strategies Cindy had researched on TL use, the team worked together to plan and test out several instructional approaches in the classroom. They introduced terminology for basic classroom phrases and instructions, including daily routines such as clarifying homework assignments, turning in papers, taking attendance, and asking for permission to use the restroom. By relying on the TL for these routines, teachers hoped to break the ice with language use and help students begin using language with a purpose. Along with new lesson content, they interspersed more repetition of previously taught language structures and expressions to help more timid students gain confidence. The teachers also worked to increase their use of visual aids to support communication without reverting back to English.

Each teacher selected five individual students to follow and observe as they implemented various lessons and activities. Prior to introducing any new strategies, the group spent time discussing each of the case study students and the particular "fears" or hesitations they observed in these individuals. To measure progress with these students, the team developed a simple rubric with four dimensions (eye contact, poise, relaxed facial expressions, and

■ Table 6.1: Target Language Communication Rubric

Date _____ Activity _____			Rating Scale 0 = Fearful/ No attempt 1 = Beginning 2 = Developing 3 = Advanced 4 = Exemplary		
Student	Eye Contact	Poise (no fidgeting)	Positive or Relaxed Facial Expression	Staying in the TL	Total Points
Student A					
Student B					
Student C					
Student D					
Student E					

staying in the TL) and rated students 0 to 4 across these four dimensions, ranging from fearful/no attempt to exemplary (see Table 6.1). For each observation episode, the teachers noted the specific classroom activity introduced and kept records of each student's response to the activity or exercise.

Several months later, the teachers reported that nearly every case study student made progress in overcoming anxiety and gaining confidence to use the TL. As Cindy explains, the process of deliberately following these case study students was enlightening for the teachers,

> As teachers, we realized we were consciously or unconsciously not calling on [these students], or avoiding including them in activities that we perceived might make them uncomfortable. Specifically observing them during activities was an eye-opener. . . . By intentionally giving them more opportunities to speak, they were becoming less fearful. In one case, a student who the teacher had previously thought would never stand and speak in front of the class, volunteered to do so and showed no visible signs of fear or discomfort while presenting a project. Using the rubric was also an inspiration for us to search out new activities, or adapt existing ones to better observe our students' responses.

For Steven, the experience not only enriched his teaching but also represented the first time in his career that he was genuinely invited to collaborate with colleagues. Early on he considered excusing himself from the process, but now he was thankful to be part of a team. Toward the end of the year, he wrote the following message to the instructional support staff:

> Sorry for taking forever for me to reply to you. The workgroup meeting has been challenging me due to several reasons, but I always feel my participation valuable because the topic/common goal in the meeting has been analyzed and shared thoughts and very thorough to contribute students learning another language than English. I'm blessed to have you as a leadership role of this, that is something I meant to say this a while ago. And I have been trying my best in my part of the team.
>
> Thank you,
>
> Steven

Although skeptical at the outset, Cindy, Michelle, and Steven made great strides in improving their practice by combining efforts to tackle a common challenge. Through focused problem solving and renewed commitment to working together, they beautifully illustrated the essence of *kyōryoku*— power being multiplied through JPA.

Key Principles for Reviving Problematic Teams

Not all cases are this successful. Helping a diverse group of teachers find common ground or getting a conflicted group to stop arguing and start working on concrete steps to improve teaching and learning is seldom as seamless and easy as the anecdotes shared in this chapter. Nevertheless, as the ongoing assistance for teams progresses across the year, leadership teams at most schools will inevitably face this challenge of planning effective assistance strategies for one or more teams characterized by unusual team chemistry, destructive dynamics, or skeptical attitudes toward collaboration and professional growth. While there are no quick and easy answers, there are five key principles that have worked in most of the cases we know about.

Find a Shared Concern

No matter how conflicted or frustrated a teacher team has become, in many cases there are persistent student achievement challenges that a majority recognize and share. When teams zeroe in on specific areas of need, and relate them to their own classrooms, it is often possible to identify one area the majority is eager to address. Once a shared goal is identified, other problems fade into the background. Some individuals may still not like each other very much, but like a sports team tired of losing, a conflicted group of teachers focusing on a shared student need can temporarily suspend old antagonisms enough to get productive collaboration going. In other cases, the shared concern becomes the glue that holds the team together despite disparate curriculum responsibilities and unique classroom contexts.

Establish Teacher Ownership

So how is a cohesive goal identified? It is vital, regardless of the student need selected, that the teachers set and share the goal themselves as they review available sources of evidence. The principal or other instructional leaders might suggest several key areas of need to choose from, but the goal chosen has to be one most teachers on a team see as immediately relevant to their own classrooms. Some examples are struggles with comprehension of expository text, understanding ratios and proportions, and writing coherent paragraphs. Once a shared problem is identified, leaders should keep at the forefront a team's commitment to work together to develop instruction. Doing something together to make a difference in everyone's classroom wins more support than talking about individual problems and leaving it to individuals to come up with answers.

Get a Commitment to Meeting Ground Rules

Making a commitment to meeting ground rules is not a new or novel concept, but taking this step seriously accomplishes two things. First, it provides a teacher team with a set of agreed-upon norms or operating principles. Second, agreeing on a set of ground rules provides everyone with license to hold colleagues accountable and run meetings in accordance with the ground rules. Here are the keys: teams establish and publish their ground rules, distribute them to everyone, and review them at strategic intervals by reflecting on meeting effectiveness.

Ground rules or norms are only a starting point. They have limited impact with the most challenging groups unless accompanied by the other key principles and supported by leadership. School leaders protect the team by removing or reducing other collaborative tasks or activities that might derail new routines and productive work.

Expect Productive Action

The middle school team featured in this chapter had spent several meetings during the previous school year carefully outlining ground rules or what they called *meeting norms,* which were still posted on the wall in the conference room during Brad's first visit:

1. What's said in-group, stays in-group.

2. Use constructive language when discussing students.

3. Talk one at a time and avoid side conversations.

4. Have the courage to confront in a constructive way.

5. Use professional language.

6. Be punctual.

7. Practice open-mindedness and forgiveness.

Despite the group's good intentions and lengthy discussions about norms, their meetings still degenerated into unproductive and often contentious battles. Why? They never transitioned from talking to action. They needed to ask themselves this question every meeting: Are we going to do something or just talk about it? When teams consistently engage in productive action, there is a corresponding shift in mindsets, beliefs, and expectations. Even the most problematic teams usually improve their attitudes and beliefs regarding collaboration if they collectively accomplish things that have a direct and positive impact on their teaching.

School leaders can mentor team facilitators to plan agendas and productively facilitate meetings that remain focused on instructional inquiry. At the same time, leaders should monitor their own behavior when joining team meetings so as not to raise other administrative topics or issues that might distract the team members from their agenda and work.

Strategize According to Teams and Individuals

Many teams will excel by establishing commitment to a shared problem, encouraging teacher ownership, setting meeting ground rules, and engaging in instructional inquiry. However, most schools will still have at least one team or a few individuals who are obstinate, unhappy, struggling, or difficult to work with, regardless of how deliberate others are about engaging in JPA.

For example, the middle school team had one teacher who was especially unhappy. She came to meetings, sat against the wall rather than joining the rest of the group at the table, made sarcastic comments, rolled her eyes, or generally refused to participate. The principal and team facilitator decided to feature her work as an example for the group to vest her with some ownership in the process. They met with the disgruntled teacher and asked for a group demonstration of her use of a graphic organizer to help students summarize main ideas and details. The teacher hesitated at first but agreed to participate and, to the group's surprise, came to the meeting fully prepared with an attitude and manner her colleagues had never witnessed. While there were still ups and downs with her meeting behavior across the year, improvement was dramatic, and the group itself gained momentum from observing this noticeable shift in the engagement and attitude of its most negative member.

Like this example, as well as the example with Steven's communication barrier, often the best and only solution for addressing these most challenging cases is to strategize one group, one individual at a time. This can seem overwhelming if all groups are struggling to work productively, but if the majority of teams move forward through a commitment to ground rules and establishing a framework for productive action, then investing this kind of focused effort on a few persistent cases becomes a more reasonable and manageable task.

Key Principles for Reviving Problematic Teams

1. Find a shared concern.
2. Establish teacher ownership.
3. Get a commitment to meeting ground rules.
4. Expect productive action.
5. Strategize according to teams and individuals.

Conclusion

As educators in both of these schools reflected on their collective efforts, they were amazed at the remarkable story of progress they had previously thought impossible. The change did not happen from increasing pressure or accountabilities, and it did not come from prolonged trust-building activities or discussion about becoming a team. The meetings came to life when they identified shared learning goals, assertively engaged in successful action, and strategically addressed key individuals. Attitudes and beliefs changed in response to new, more productive behaviors, galvanizing faculty with renewed hope and confidence in the power of collaboration.

Behind each story of productive collaboration, like those shared in this chapter, there are additional stories of individual teachers tirelessly working to improve their craft and maximize learning opportunities for children and youth. In many cases, teachers continue this pursuit despite persuasive reasons to give up. In the next chapter, we celebrate six compelling examples of teachers who inspired others through their courageous commitment to teaching, unwavering compassion for students, and enduring focus on improvement.

REFLECTION QUESTIONS

KEY PRINCIPLE: *Power is multiplied to the fullest extent when we work together productively.*

1. How does engaging in productive activity change the dynamics of the collaborative process?

2. What is the focus of conversations in your collaborative settings? Do these conversations reflect JPA?

3. If you play a role supporting collaborative work in your school or district, which of your teams struggle with challenges similar to those described in this chapter? Reflecting on the five "Key Principles for Reviving Problematic Teams," how might you help them refocus their work?

ADDITIONAL RESOURCES

- See Leader's Guide in the Appendix for additional team exercises from this chapter and presentation ideas for the "JPA" portrait.
- Visit the companion website to download presentation slides, including a full color digital image of the portrait. Also find customizable templates, checklists, and tools to assist your implementation efforts.

Available at http://www.corwin.com/ErmelingTeachingBetter

REFERENCES

This chapter was adapted from previously published work in the following:

Ermeling, B. A. (2012). Breathe new life into collaboration: 5 principles for reviving problematic groups. *The Learning Principal, 8*(1), 1, 4–6. Adapted with permission from Learning Forward, http://www.learningforward.org. All rights reserved.

Ermeling, B. A., & Gallimore, R. (2013). Learning to be a community: Schools need adaptable models to create successful programs. *Journal of Staff Development (JSD), 34*(2), 42–45. Adapted with permission from Learning Forward, http://www.learningforward.org. All rights reserved.

CHAPTER 7

Remaining Stubborn for a Long Time

Six Practitioner Stories of Courage and Persistence

5000 Reasons to Quit

KEY PRINCIPLE

The pursuit of teaching better is an arduous race demanding courage and commitment to remain stubborn for a long time.

Painting by high school student artist, Chelsea Madden, 2015. ©2015 Brad & Genevieve Ermeling.

PORTRAIT #7: 5000
Reasons to Quit

During the 2004 U.S. Olympic Track and Field Trials in Sacramento, California, Genevieve qualified to compete in both the 1500 and 5000 meters. She was 33 years old at the time and had just rediscovered competitive running in 2002. The trials marked the culmination of a surprising resurgence in her career after spending seven years away from the sport to serve as a teacher in Japan.

The 5000 meters was scheduled for Friday evening with the 1500 slated for the following week, but on Tuesday she pulled her hamstring. The injury came during the seventh of 10 quarter-mile repeats, one of her last training workouts prior to the event. The final announcement she had qualified came on Wednesday just two days before the trials. "The voice on the other line said she was a volunteer from USA Track and Field," Genevieve recalls. "She told me I was going to be entered in the Olympic Trials 5000 meters." Hoping her leg would respond for just one more race, she rested on Thursday, warmed up on Friday, wore a protective sleeve around her hamstring, and lined up for the competition (Kuehls, 2004).

She looked comfortable at the start and kept pace with the pack for the first several laps, but as the race progressed, her hamstring would not respond. Near the top of the stadium on the east side of the track, Brad sat nervously on the bleachers watching the race unfold. Each time she passed this section of the stands, Brad stood and yelled out "*Ganbare*"—a cheer he knew would distinguish his voice in the midst of the large crowd. *Ganbare* is a Japanese term commonly used to encourage and inspire others in competition or in times of adversity. The typical English translation is "keep fighting" or "give it your all," but these words fail to capture the full essence of the term in Japanese culture. A more direct translation of the *kanji* characters would be "stand firm" or "remain stubborn for a long time." This call for perseverance is expressed with a deep sense of togetherness and collective resolve: "We are sharing in your pain and struggle; we are standing firm with you and behind you." This was the spirit and mood of the stadium that night as Genevieve rounded each of the 12.5 laps.

Lap after lap, despite a growing gap between her and the other runners, she kept pushing herself to continue. The Sacramento crowd began to notice the effort and a wave of applause followed her around the track, each section of the stadium taking turns to stand and cheer as she persevered through the final 1200 meters. The spontaneous reaction of the crowd was emotional to witness. As she neared his section for the final lap, Brad fought through tears to yell "*Ganbare*" one last time.

After Genevieve crossed the finish line, she bent double; the hamstring seized up because it was no longer in use. "I had about four good laps," she told a *Runner's World* journalist. "The rest was pretty tough." She also said she considered dropping out because she knew "the time I was going to run . . . people in high school run that. Was that worthy of the Olympic Trials?"

But she didn't drop out. She fought off each internal voice that was telling her to quit and mustered the strength to fight on.

Teaching can be a demanding and sometimes even discouraging task. External pressures, time constraints, diverse learning needs, challenging curriculum, difficult relationships, and a lack of support or affirmation are just some of the daily challenges educators face. Perhaps most importantly, improvements in teaching do not come quickly or easily. Discernible improvements substantiated by student results emerge gradually and incrementally over months and years of sustained effort. Teaching requires courage: courage to uphold standards and convictions, courage to self-examine and embrace shortcomings, and courage to remain committed in the face of difficult conditions. Teaching is a bold act of optimism that one's efforts can truly matter for students (Nater & Gallimore, 2010; Saunders & Ermeling, 2009).

In our research and observations, we are continually inspired by encounters with educators who exemplify this lifelong commitment to improvement and the resiliency to overcome obstacles. Whether veterans or first-year teachers, inner city or rural contexts, public or private institutions, entry-level or advanced placement courses, poor or middle-class communities, we find committed educators engaged in the often invisible work of improving their craft. This final chapter highlights four prominent examples from our interviews and correspondence with teachers representing this wide continuum of classroom environments, followed by two inspiring examples from another teaching context. With the exception of the last two stories, all school and teacher names are pseudonyms.

Paula Fernandez—Special Education Teacher

Paula Fernandez was a veteran special education teacher. She worked at a large, urban middle school in a poor and working-class community with a 95 percent Latino student body. The school had failed to meet Adequate Yearly Progress targets for the last five years and was under pressure from the state for corrective action. Teachers were inundated with professional development programs and "turnaround" initiatives, which were hastily implemented with little coherence or support for teacher learning.

For the past seven months, something different lifted the spirit of the special education teachers. District and school leadership set aside time and established a system of ongoing assistance to help them launch a collaborative inquiry project to study their teaching. Teachers provided input on configuration of teams, and Paula volunteered to serve as facilitator to lead her group through the process. The team's experience was so powerful and so compelling that other faculty started to express interest, and the principal began making plans for school-wide implementation. Sadly, just as they were picking up momentum, the district announced severe cutbacks in spending, including training and support for professional development.

Emboldened by their collective experience and renewed commitment to continuous learning, Paula penned the following letter to the district superintendent.

> Mr. [Superintendent]:
>
> This letter is to add a teacher's perspective . . . to your information base as you strive to make the best decision possible regarding [programs] for the benefit of our students.
>
> Our Special Education Team at Franklin Middle School successfully completed our first [instructional inquiry] cycle. As teachers, we learned the power that comes from collaboration. Our lesson was built from the combined knowledge of the content, our collective skills as educators, and our shared understanding of the special students we served. The results were better than we could hope. Ninety percent of our students obtained the desired outcome.
>
> More important than the numbers were our observations of the individual results. You should have seen the face of my little

Jesse—who struggles mightily—light up with understanding. In fact, he got a near perfect score. The other teachers in the group reported similar experiences.

The training and support I received as a facilitator helped me develop a climate of cooperation and consensus that made these results possible. Furthermore, the experience is helping me become a more active and vocal participant of my own professional development. The support we have received as teachers encouraged us to pursue the opportunity . . . as professionals researching and evaluating our own practice.

I understand that the district is suffering under the pressure of our economic climate. However, I'd like you to please consider that good professional development is crucial to the success of our students. [This] has been the best professional development experience I have had in my teaching career.

Thank you for your consideration.

Paula Fernandez

Paula's voice was heard, the program was extended, and several years later, Franklin Middle School successfully expanded this collaborative work to every teacher and subject area. Paula's spirit of persistence, passion for improving her practice, and courage to advocate for colleagues and students inspired a community of educators, influenced districts leaders, and galvanized a multiyear investment in continuous improvement.

Maria Alvarez—English as a Second Language Teacher

Maria Alvarez was an English as a second language (ESL) teacher at a middle school in a poor, industrial neighborhood adjacent to a busy interstate. The school faced many challenges including discipline problems, a history of low achievement, and a high percentage of English learners. In an effort to focus more intently on teaching and learning, the administration had recently acquired district funds to compensate after-school professional learning and made a serious commitment to protect regular settings for teacher collaboration.

As an example of their commitment, just an hour before one team meeting, a traffic accident smashed a car through the side of the building where teachers met for collaborative planning. When they arrived and found a wrecked car sitting in the middle of the room, there was no discussion of canceling the meeting. Teachers consulted with the assistant principal about an alternative meeting space, quickly relocated to the library, and went on with their scheduled business for collective inquiry and instructional improvement.

Working in this collaborative context, Maria and four of her colleagues became members of a vertical ESL team, each responsible for different levels of the ESL curriculum. Maria taught the entry-level classes. The team met biweekly to plan, implement, and reflect on lessons, using student work samples to measure progress with pressing student needs. The group was especially concerned with the lack of coherent paragraph structure observed in the majority of student writing samples, a persistent problem they faced for several years. Among other things, the group found that students composed journal entries as if they were telling oral stories. Students were more apt to connect sentences with conjunctions (mostly "ands") rather than end a sentence, punctuate it, and start a new sentence with a capital letter.

Focusing on the entry-level course, the team spent several months planning lessons to help students distinguish between short dependent clauses that should be joined with conjunctions and longer independent clauses that should be separated into two or more sentences. They increased the number of journal entries and asked students to pause and analyze sentences, determining when clauses should be combined or separated. They projected example entries in front of class, so students could identify run-on sentences and suggest improvements. They also read aloud sample entries, asking students to listen for fragments that should be connected.

Throughout this period, teachers continued meeting regularly to study writing samples, adjust teaching methods, and implement refinements. After several months of persistent work with combining and separating clauses, the team started to see significant results. By January, 90 percent of Maria's students were composing sentences with appropriate length, improved discretion for joining and separating clauses, effective use of conjunctions, and proper end punctuation. Maria immediately shared the news with her colleagues and expressed how amazing it was to see her students composing coherent paragraphs.

During the next team reflection meeting, Maria talked about the significance of these results as well as her gratitude for the collaborative experience:

In the intro level, [learning when to join or separate clauses] is a big achievement because now they are writing paragraphs. . . . I don't get these long paragraphs with the "and . . . and" and never ending sentence. Now I have short sentences and I see a lot of periods and capital letters . . . .

This is the first time I am part of a community . . . a real community. . . . We share lesson plans and we share ideas and we share materials. For me it was really really helpful. Because now I know that what I'm doing is not going to be wasted. It's not going to be lost. I know someone else [at the next level] is going to take over and is going to continue doing the same job. And I know that everything I do is appreciated so it makes me feel good. And being together and talking about it really makes us feel like it's not only my problem, this is everyone's problem and we can get together and try to solve it.

After years of frustration with student writing, teachers started to focus more intently on small, systematic changes over time and started to support each other with challenges across their vertical curriculum assignments. The results they experienced with paragraph writing boosted the team's confidence and strengthened their resolve to tackle the next instructional challenge. Maria emphasized:

We need to continue. We need to continue. Because communication is very important. We are working for the same group of kids. Sooner or later they are going to be in our classroom, so it's important that we continue with our work.

Like the stadium crowd watching the 5000 meters, the ESL team's example inspired members of the school community as well as other teams and instructional leaders throughout the district. The assistant principal described the impact:

I remember when [the team leader] told me you got 90 percent, how excited we all got. Not only us, even down at the district. It gives me a sense of meaning. . . . It's a highlight of my life sometimes when I can come here and I listen to you folks discuss meaningful problems. We're doing something important . . . and it's been reflected in your classroom. I can see the difference.

Tom Richards—Science Teacher

Tom Richards (a member of the lesson study team described in Chapter 3) taught high school science for 35 years. For the last 30 years, he taught regular and advanced chemistry courses at the same suburban high school. Tom's passion for science, commitment to his craft, and obvious concern for students brought him great admiration and respect throughout the school community. More than 90 percent of Tom's students consistently passed the annual advanced placement (AP) exam, something he humbly attributed to the many talented students he was blessed to teach. Despite a successful career, strong reputation, and well-established library of resources and lesson plans, Tom was never interested in coasting. He approached each new year with a sense of stewardship and emphasized being faithful with the responsibility of helping students develop scientific knowledge and skills.

When we first approached him with the opportunity to participate in a lesson study research project, Tom embraced the challenge and assisted us in recruiting other members of his department. He expressed significant anxiety about being videotaped and observed by his colleagues but believed this would be a valuable way for the team to reflect and improve their practice. Most importantly, Tom viewed this project as an opportunity to deepen his own understanding and skills for facilitating inquiry teaching. Like other members of the group, his first attempts required some adjustments to existing instructional routines and some "pain," as he described it, observing students' responses to the open-ended struggle activities.

> The other "aha" that was a little bit painful for me was to see how much misconception they had about a lot of these topics (laughter). Things that I thought I had taught them, at least under those circumstances they weren't bringing them to bear. They might have known them in one context but not in the context I was having them apply them.

In the second iteration of lessons, our reflection and planning discussions for Amy's biology lab inspired ideas for a calorimetry discovery lab, where Tom asked students to both design their own lab procedures and carry out the experiment. During the first half of the lesson, he carefully scaffolded this effort by giving students opportunities for feedback and correction before proceeding with the experiment (to ensure safety with the lab chemicals). During the second half of the lesson, he encouraged students' independent efforts to test out their procedures and report their own findings. Tom spoke of this with great satisfaction, describing how wonderful it was to watch students engaged in true science.

> In the early 60s the big push was toward inquiry, and that's what my whole life in science teaching has been trying to push, is to get kids to discover stuff on their own, especially during lab work. The process that traditionally we have done has been that the teacher designs the procedures that will lead them to discover stuff. Which is pretty high-level lab work, instead of just a cookbook approach where you say, "Do this so that you can discover that." You as a teacher draw up the guidelines for what you want the students to do. But what we did [in these lessons] is we've given them a problem and say, "Now, you design the procedure to do it," which is really a different twist. I like that a lot. . . . The assumption was originally that, "Well, maybe they don't know." Or maybe, "Let's not waste time having them grope about. Just lead them in this direction." I think the [teaching approaches] that are truest to the definition of what science is, is doing inquiry to the deepest level you can push it.

After 35 years of teaching, this lesson marked the first time Tom had asked students to design their own procedures for a scientific lab. He had every reason to be complacent with past achievements but instead pushed himself and his students to deeper levels of inquiry. Energized by this experience, he began mapping out ideas for the next round of improvement—teaching students to generate their own hypotheses.

> What I hope that we could do in the future would be to give them a problem and say, "You think about what's the hypothesis you're trying to test, and now you design the procedure to do it, and then you test it." I think that would be even a higher level, which is really what science research is all about.

Doug Wilson—Math Teacher

Doug Wilson was a middle school and high school math teacher whose story is a bit different from the others. We chose to include Doug here as one example of the dedicated, individual improvement efforts of teachers who persist with their own inquiry and growth even without the benefits of a collaborative context.

After several years working in a shipping office and completing graduate school, Doug began his education career as a middle school teacher. He taught math for English learners in an underprivileged, densely urban community with a transient immigrant population and daily threats of gang violence. Doug observed firsthand the tragic circumstances students faced in this unstable environment. One student died from a drug overdose. Several students brought guns or knives to school for protection during their walks home. Thirteen-year old girls faced tough decisions with unwanted pregnancies. Most didn't even have access to basic health or dental care. Several of his students were fitted with glasses for the first time when Doug and his colleagues arranged for a charity organization to provide site-based eye exams. Doug had every reason to lower expectations and blame outside influences for low achievement results, but he kept working to make a difference.

> It's just a lot of passing the buck and not being willing to take on challenges. . . . It's always tempting to say, "They can't do this or they can't do that. They don't do anything at home and they don't work." The parents are sending you the best kids they have. . . . I can't control what happens outside of the classroom, but I can control what happens inside the classroom.

In his second teaching assignment, Doug worked as a high school teacher for a diverse population of students in another part of the county. He taught algebra to *repeaters*—students who had previously failed the course one or more times. Having failed eighth grade algebra himself, Doug empathized with students and worked to help them rebuild confidence. He brought high expectations, a fresh perspective, and some unconventional ideas. For example, when assigning homework, Doug provided a list of answers along with assigned problems and gave students credit for self-assessing which problems they struggled with. This allowed him to diagnose learning needs and promptly address specific challenges during the same class period. He also allowed students to take tests as many times as needed to demonstrate mastery, providing different problems and questions for the same topics and standards.

During the first day of class, Doug emphasized that math was just a vehicle they were using to learn success skills for life.

> I told them, "I've been in your seat. I know what it feels like. I know what it feels like when what you're being taught doesn't make sense . . . ." At the beginning of class each year, I asked

students to write the following on the front of their notebooks: "I'm not bad at math. I have just had negative experiences in math. This is not a math class. This is a class for success training."

At the end of this first class period, Doug also asked students to begin writing a math autobiography.

Stubbornly searching for every opportunity to help students succeed, Doug decided there was more he could do—even outside of class. He decided to launch a math workshop for parents.

> I was thinking, "I knew these were all students who had failed algebra at least once. I bet the parents don't know the first thing about what they are doing, or questions to ask them, or how to help them." And I also thought that if kids who were failing or had failed were seeing their parents make this kind of effort, it would be motivating. . . . I wanted to go beyond parental involvement to engagement. I wanted to do actual authentic parent learning . . . in a very concrete, hands-on, conceptual way to help them understand the concepts that students would be wrestling with.

Doug describes his initial conversation with the school principal as skeptical but supportive. After listening to Doug's proposal, the principal cautioned, "OK, two things: (1) No one has ever done this before here, and (2) no one's going to show up." Doug was undeterred in his response, "OK, two things: (1) If no one shows up, I'll get some grading done, and (2) I need the bathrooms open."

Doug organized two evening sessions per month for parents and sent out invitations through the school e-mail system. About 20 percent of parents participated each month. Some expressed hesitancy and even fear about their math abilities, but Doug convinced them to come and give it a try. They worked with algebra tiles, function machines, graphing calculators, and other materials the students would be using. Parents initially expressed frustration with the conceptual challenges, but Doug patiently encouraged them to stick with it: "I hear you loud and clear. I promise that before you leave today, you'll feel a lot better about that topic or about that problem. You just have to trust me."

The response from parents and administration was overwhelmingly positive, and word spread to other parents and faculty. Best of all, students of these parents showed significant progress on regular math assessments. Several students went from far below basic in eighth grade to proficient and even advanced by the end of the course. Doug explains, "The principal and other faculty couldn't believe I had repeaters performing as advanced."

Reflecting on this example, Doug described the motivation for his relentless attitude and the mindset required to keep improving in the face of obstacles.

> What kept me going is, I love the subject, and I wanted people to have the breakthrough I had, going from failing to actually majoring in [mathematics]. . . . You have to make the commitment to being really reflective and honest with yourself. You have to hold a mirror up to what you're doing. You have to be willing to attribute some of students' success and failure to your instruction. . . . You have to believe that small changes can have an effect over time.

One final example comes from another teaching context—a pair of coaches who preferred to be known as "teachers." The first is a legend, the second, his pupil. Together they tell an inspiring story of longevity, perseverance, and unwavering commitment to teaching better.

John Wooden—Basketball Teacher

Coach John Wooden "taught" basketball at UCLA from 1948 to 1975. His men's basketball teams earned 10 National Collegiate Athletic Association (NCAA) titles in 12 years, reeled off an 88-game win streak, and won 38 straight tournament games. He was named NCAA Coach of the Year six times and Men's College Coach of the 20th Century by both the Naismith Hall of Fame and ESPN. But few people know that Wooden coached 15 seasons at UCLA before winning his first championship.

Throughout his extraordinary career, Coach Wooden insisted that much of what he did to teach basketball he learned as a high school English teacher in the 1930s (Ermeling, 2012). Wooden credits his success to slow, steady, consistent efforts to improve his teaching.

> When you improve a little each day, eventually big things occur. . . . Not tomorrow, not the next day, but eventually a big gain is made. Don't look for the big, quick improvement. Seek the small improvement one day at a time. That's the only way it happens— and when it happens, it lasts. (Wooden & Jamison, 1997, p. 143)

Wooden emphasized that the 15 seasons before his first championship were no less successful. He didn't teach any differently. He just kept learning and expanding his knowledge. He believed that teaching can always be improved and that dedicated teachers and coaches should never stop trying to get better. During every year of his career, regardless of his success, he identified an area of his teaching that he thought needed improvement. Based on his research each off-season, he developed and tried out various instructional adjustments, took notes during practices, and refined his practice lessons until he was satisfied that players were progressing. He thought anyone who is "through learning, is through" (Nater & Gallimore, 2010).

Wooden was also incredibly generous and willing to share his knowledge with any young teacher or coach who reached out to him for guidance and advice. In fact, Wooden's knowledge and advice saved at least one high school coach's career. The story of what this coach learned and its effects on his teaching provides another rich example of steady, relentless, continual improvement.

Hank Bias—Basketball Teacher

In 2003, Henry "Hank" Bias, head boys' basketball coach (and physical education teacher) at Fairmont High School in Kettering, Ohio, had just finished his third consecutive losing season and was profoundly discouraged by his team's 3–17 record. He questioned whether he had what it takes to coach basketball and mulled changing careers.

A deflated Bias contemplated graduate school and contacted Professor George DeMarco at the University of Dayton, who urged him to do some research on coaching. One of the articles he recommended was a study of Wooden's pedagogy based on live observations of practice sessions in 1975. Bias was intrigued and contacted one of the researchers, Ron Gallimore, to ask if he had any films of Wooden coaching. The answer was yes, but Hank would need the coach's permission to borrow them, so Ron provided John Wooden's home phone number.

After some initial hesitation, Hank mustered the courage to dial Wooden's number. As he started to leave a message, Wooden picked up and said hello. Hank began to explain that he was a high school basketball coach in the Dayton area and had some questions about teaching the game of basketball. Wooden interrupted and started asking questions himself. To

Hank's surprise and delight, they talked for 20 minutes about teaching basketball and how to improve as a coach.

Considering an individual inquiry project? See the companion website: "Suggestions for Conducting Individual Inquiry With a Mentor (http://www.corwin.com/ErmelingTeachingBetter).

Coach Wooden invited Hank to come visit him, so they could discuss coaching and teaching at length. A few days later, Bias was sitting in Wooden's condo, surrounded by countless mementos and memorabilia. Wooden shared many bits of advice, but one of the most important was that better instruction was the answer Hank was seeking, and the way to get it was to relentlessly and continuously work on improving teaching, one practice session after another. Hank went back to Ohio and began following Wooden's advice immediately.

The first season after he met with Wooden, Hank's team doubled its win total, finishing 6–15. The team improved again the next year, nearly hitting .500 at 9–11. In the third year of Hank's efforts to become a better teacher, the Firebirds' record was 17–6. Fairmont won the conference championship, and Bias won a local coach-of-the-year award.

In the five seasons after Hank began implementing Wooden's lessons, Fairmont's winning percentage was 62 percent, compared to 29 percent in the seasons prior to Hank's meeting Wooden. All of this was accomplished with no significant improvement in talent level and during a period where the surrounding competition was arguably tougher.

Much like Coach Wooden's success, Hank's story can sound almost magical as if written for a Hollywood script, but behind the scenes, Hank's story (like Wooden's) was one of steady effort toward continuous, incremental improvement. Hank systematically followed the same sequence of inquiry steps: identifying a problem or topic to research and study, preparing and implementing detailed plans, utilizing evidence to drive reflection, and persistently working toward detectable improvements.

Hank described a number of key insights he gained from these ongoing improvement efforts. He learned to make better use of practice time, to use concise and disciplined instructional talk, to organize drills that simulate gamelike decision-making opportunities, to differentiate support for individual players, and to document notes after each practice to see how he could improve.

Most importantly, Hank learned to measure success as Wooden defined it: "peace of mind, which is a direct result of self-satisfaction in knowing you made the effort to do your best to become the best that you are capable of becoming" (Nater & Gallimore, 2010, p. 25).

Back to the Track

Wooden's definition of success is the same way Genevieve measured her performance in the 5000 meters. After 12.5 long laps around the Sacramento stadium, her race concluded, but the story didn't end there.

As she limped off the track behind the other runners, she received the most validating compliment of all from a fellow competitor in the back of the pack. Jennifer Kramer had finished second to last in their heat but was still more than a minute ahead. When Genevieve exited the track, Jennifer met her and asked one simple question: "Did you finish?" The answer was the affirmative. And then Kramer said, "Good job" (Kuehls, 2004). As Genevieve continued walking in the dark behind the stadium, people kept stopping her to say that her race inspired them. "I realized that the effort was worthy—even if my finishing time wasn't," she recalls.

The day after the 5000 meters, while visiting with other members of the running community, we met a man who had attended the race the night before and joined in the wave of applause that spread through the stadium during Genevieve's final laps. The man told Genevieve that he was suffering from cancer and that watching her finish the race gave him the courage to keep fighting through his battle with disease.

Like these words of affirmation and the wave of applause that spread through the Sacramento stadium, the stories in this chapter serve as a reminder to all educators that you are not alone in this pursuit. Thousands of educators are running the same race each day in their classrooms and persisting to improve teaching and learning. It would be so easy to stop running, to give up on the cause, to step off the track, but they don't. They keep learning, and they keep improving. They keep setting goals. They keep reflecting. They remain stubborn for a long time.

Like the 5000 meters, the work of improving teaching is neither a quick sprint nor recreational jog. It is an arduous race demanding patience and commitment. There may be 5000 reasons to quit, but much greater reward and satisfaction that come from persisting with the process and embracing each new challenge as an opportunity for *teaching better.*

REFLECTION QUESTIONS

KEY PRINCIPLE: *The pursuit of teaching better is an arduous race demanding courage and commitment to remain stubborn for a long time.*

1. Which of the stories in this chapter did you find encouraging? What aspect of the story specifically resonated with you?

2. This chapter describes teaching as a "bold act of optimism"? What kind of courage does teaching require for you?

3. Where do you find inspiration to remain focused and committed to instructional improvement? How often do you take time to encourage your colleagues?

4. In what ways might your school or community recognize the courage and commitment of teachers? How might you celebrate small steps toward big goals?

ADDITIONAL RESOURCES

- See Leader's Guide in the Appendix for additional team exercises from this chapter and presentation ideas for the "5000 Reasons to Quit" portrait.
- Visit the companion website to download presentation slides, including a full color digital image of the portrait. Also find customizable templates, checklists, and tools to assist your implementation efforts.

Available at http://www.corwin.com/ErmelingTeachingBetter

REFERENCES

Ermeling, B. A. (2012). Improving teaching through continuous learning: The inquiry process John Wooden used to become coach of the century. *Quest, 64*, 197–208.

Kuehls, D. (2004). 5000 reasons to quit. *Runner's World* (Online edition.).

Nater, S., & Gallimore, R. (2010). *You haven't taught until they have learned: John Wooden's teaching principles and practices.* Morgantown, WV: Fitness International Technology.

Saunders, W., & Ermeling, B.A. (2009). *Learning teams: Instructional leadership manual.* Glenview, IL: Pearson.

Wooden, J., & Jamison, S. (1997). *Wooden: A lifetime of observations and reflections on and off the court.* Lincolnwood, IL: Contemporary.

Some portions of this chapter were adapted from previously published work in the following:

Gallimore, R., Ermeling, B. A., & Nater, S. (2012, February/March). Timeless lessons: Encouraging your coaches to take a page from the Wizard of Westwood can turn them into teachers, and have a profound effect. *Athletic Management.* Adapted with permission from *Athletic Management,* http://www.athleticmanagement.com All rights reserved.

Appendix •———

Leader's Guide to Improvement Portraits

This guide provides practical suggestions for educational leaders to incorporate the improvement portraits and key principles in large-group presentations and team discussions. The notes and ideas are primarily designed for the building level but can also be adapted for system-level leaders working to effect change at the building level. Possible use cases include professional development seminars, faculty meetings, leadership team meetings, principal training events, teacher team meetings, university courses, and teacher induction settings.

Unlike a manual or handbook, these suggestions and resources need not be implemented in a linear sequence. Rather, the starting point depends primarily on local school context and specific implementation needs. For example, leaders at one school already underway with collaborative inquiry, but struggling to effectively mobilize leadership and assistance, might begin with the key principle and practical resources in Chapter 5. Leaders at another school, working to effectively structure newly established settings for collaborative inquiry, might focus attention on Chapter 3. And leaders at yet another school, seeking to revive problematic groups through joint productive activity, might focus on Chapter 6. As needs change and implementation cycles progress over a period of years, leaders can continue incorporating additional portraits and content that best align with their immediate priorities.

The following section outlines specific presentation ideas and suggested team exercises for each of the seven chapters and improvement portraits. A companion set of digital resources, including metaphor descriptions, presentation slides, and full-color images for each portrait, are also available on the book website (http://www.corwin.com/ErmelingTeachingBetter).

Portrait #1: Rotting Ship at Sea

Presentation Idea: Use the "Rotting Ship at Sea" portrait to launch a new school year of collaborative inquiry or lesson study work. Introduce the metaphor and the importance of balancing urgency with intentionality. While identifying school-wide or individual team inquiry goals, refer to these goals as the next "plank we are investigating" as we continue to stabilize the "ship." School and team leaders can continue referencing the metaphor throughout the year while helping teams develop patience with steady, incremental improvement of teaching.

Team Exercise: After presenting the portrait, ask your leadership team or teacher team to discuss some of the challenges of balancing urgency with intentionality. Identify scenarios from your own school or classrooms where you experience tension between these two concepts, such as rushing ahead with technology integration without a specific plan for how it will support learning opportunities. Strategize on steps you can take to place more emphasis on intentional study and effective use. (Download the "Balancing Urgency and Intentionality Reflection Exercise" from the companion website.)

Portrait #2: Rich Drop of Food Coloring

Presentation Idea: Use the "Rich Drop of Food Coloring" portrait to teach the benefits of steady, concentrated effort with planning and analysis of individual lessons. Bring in a large container of water, and demonstrate the ripple effect by releasing a few ordinary drops of water into the container (representing superficial study of teaching and generic professional development). Then use a drop of blue or green food coloring to demonstrate the rich, permeating effect of the instructional inquiry process.

Alternatively, divide the room into small groups, each situated at a table with a cylindrical container of water, a science lab pipet, and a small bottle of blue or green food coloring. Beginning with the pipet and ordinary drops of plain water, provide prompts to guide groups through the experiment. Ask them to stop, record, and discuss observations for both the plain drops of water and the drop of food coloring. Depending on available time, either provide prompts for group discussion, or give a short presentation on the contrast between short-lived episodes of professional development and sustained opportunities for instructional inquiry. Use observational evidence from the two experiments to frame the discussion or explanation.

Team Exercise: After presenting the portrait, ask your leadership team or teacher team to read and discuss the essential skills and mindsets highlighted in our firsthand account of Japanese lesson study (fashioning a coherent storyline, articulating and testing hypotheses, relying on evidence to guide reflection, embracing collaboration and collective ownership of improvement, and persisting with problems over time). As a group, describe each element in your own words. Then, individually reflect on each of the elements using the following notation system:

- Write a "+" next to items for "we do this well."
- Write a "–" next to items for "aware of this but could be more intentional."
- Write a "!" next to items for "something we need to work on."

Following individual reflection, discuss your answers as a group, and consider specific next steps for addressing areas of need. (Download the "Essential Skills and Mindsets Reflection Exercise" from the companion website.)

Portrait #3: Japanese Toothpick (*Tsumayōji*)

Presentation Idea: Use the "Japanese Toothpick (*Tsumayōji*)" illustration to teach the power of expanding horizons of observation and seeing that something can be completely different. These toothpicks can be purchased online at Amazon by searching for *Japanese toothpicks*. A container of 500 toothpicks is less than $5. Distribute a Western-style toothpick and a Japanese toothpick to each attendee. Have them analyze and consider the difference. Then teach them the unique design of the Japanese toothpick. Close by emphasizing the symbolic message and key improvement principle.

Team Exercise: After presenting the portrait, ask your leadership team or teacher team to read and discuss the section on conditions that enabled collaborative improvement from the high school science case study (stable settings, facilitated inquiry, recursive process focused on improving teaching, and observing and reflecting on lessons). As a group, describe each element in your own words. Then, individually reflect on each of the elements using the following notation system:

- Write a "+" next to items for "we do this well."
- Write a "–" next to items for "aware of this but could be more intentional."
- Write a "!" next to items for "something we need to work on."

Following individual reflection, discuss your answers as a group, and consider specific next steps for addressing areas of need. (Download the "Collaborative Improvement Reflection Exercise" from the companion website.)

Portrait #4: Virtual Treasure Chest

Presentation Idea: Use the "Virtual Treasure Chest" portrait to introduce several example digital libraries that teacher teams might access during their inquiry work (see examples provided in Chapter 4). Describe the image of a treasure chest, which signifies the collection and preservation of hard-won assets. When something is of value, enthusiasts who recognize its worth seek it out, study its history, and make it publicly available for others who will appreciate its unique origin, utility, and purpose. Share the quote from Dewey and the unfortunate reality that most of the hard-won assets of teachers are never shared or accessed by others. Then introduce the examples of inquiry-based digital libraries as invaluable tools for deepening professional knowledge and stretching beyond what we already know.

As an alternative, also consider using the "Virtual Treasure Chest" to introduce a webpage or portal on the school, district, or third-party website, where teacher teams can upload their latest work on instructional inquiry, comment, discuss, and share findings. Describe the website or portal as a dynamic access point to preserve and retrieve these resources, so they might benefit next year's learners, so they might stimulate inquiry for other practitioners, and so they might be refined and adapted for learners in other contexts.

Team Exercise: After presenting the portrait, ask your leadership team or teacher team to reflect on a time in their careers when they figured out how to address a particular teaching and learning problem—some aspect of the curriculum they were trying to help students understand or master—and the insight they gained about how to teach it well. Ask them to be as specific as possible.

- What was the learning goal you were persistently working to address?
- What was the pivotal nuance in your delivery of instruction that opened up a learning opportunity for students?

Take several minutes to write individually. Then share your discovery stories as a group.

Discussion topics could include the following:

- How does the collaborative instructional inquiry process enable more deliberate discovery of these insights (treasures of teacher knowledge)?
- What opportunities are available for your school community to seek out new knowledge and alternative approaches? What opportunities do you have for generating and contributing knowledge for other practitioners? How might you improve these opportunities?

(Download the "Teaching Discovery Reflection Exercise" from the companion website.)

Portrait #5: Winter Horseshoes

Presentation Idea: Use the "Winter Horseshoes" portrait to emphasize the importance of matching bold strategies and ideas with attention to detail. Provide specific examples of details that will need to be addressed for collaborative inquiry to be successful in your school or district context. To demonstrate mutual commitment and reciprocal accountability, describe the details that school leaders will make a commitment to address (e.g., meet regularly to inventory and discuss support needs of each team, protect settings and avoid distracting teams with other administrative tasks, etc.). Possibly share the slide of the Triadic Model to demonstrate this commitment and support structure. Then also describe the details that teachers will need to address so that teams can maximize the benefit of collaborative inquiry settings (e.g. be on time, complete work between meetings, take time to record and complete lesson plans, preserve copies of student work, etc.).

Team Exercise: With your leadership team or teacher team, read over the winter horseshoes metaphor description. Discuss some of the "winter horseshoes" that are being neglected and might potentially cripple your instructional improvement efforts. (Download the "Winter Horseshoes Reflection Exercise" from the companion website.)

Triadic Model Exercise: With your leadership team, read the section on the Triadic Model of assistance, and discuss implications for your own school context. What aspects of the Triadic Model are in place at our school? What settings are missing? How could you make time for these settings? Are you focused on distal or proximal settings? What leadership roles need to be created or changed to make this happen? What links between settings need to be strengthened? (Download the "Triadic Model Exercise" from the companion website.)

Assistance Matrix Exercise: As a leadership team, collectively discuss the process for designing and using an Assistance Matrix. Download the "Assistance Matrix Exercise" from the companion website, and locate the link for the Google Sheet template. Then follow the six steps outlined in the chapter to begin strategically coordinating and distributing meaningful assistance across multiple teams (e.g., customize settings and contact points, determine and record strategic assistance plans for each team, etc.).

KTL Summary Pilot Exercise: As a leadership team, discuss how well you know your teams' stories. Do you know them well enough to identify gaps in their planning, knowledge, or judgment? Inventory each of your teams. Which of them might serve as a productive pilot opportunity for coauthoring a KTL Summary? Have each team leader pick one group and test out the process for one cycle of inquiry. (Refer to Chapter 5 for a description of the process, detailed examples, and recommended components of an effective summary. Download the "KTL Summary Pilot Exercise" from the companion website.)

Portrait #6: Joint Productive Activity (JPA)

Presentation Idea: Use the "JPA" portrait to make the important distinction between productive, focused collaboration and loosely defined, unstructured collaboration. Project the digital image of the portrait, and introduce the Japanese word for *collaboration*. Explain the meaning of each Chinese character as outlined in the presentation slide and metaphor description (*cooperation* and *power*). Ask if anyone sees a relationship between the two characters. After allowing for one or two responses, follow by explaining how power is contained three times in the character for *cooperation* and the cross-like symbol on the left implies "the fullest extent." Provide the complete meaning of the word: in Japanese, the word for *collaboration* means "power is multiplied to the fullest extent when we work together productively."

Team Exercise: After presenting the portrait, ask your leadership team to discuss where the teams in your school fall on the continuum between joint productive collaboration and loosely defined, unstructured collaboration.

Use the "Reviving Problematic Groups Reflection Exercise" on the companion website to review and prioritize actions that will better support or and/or revitalize unproductive or problematic teams you have identified.

Portrait #7: 5000 Reasons to Quit

Presentation Idea: Consider launching an annual "5000 Reasons to Quit" award to honor a teacher or a teacher team who has gone the extra mile to improve practice and create learning opportunities for students. During the inaugural year, project the improvement portrait and read the "5000 Reasons to Quit" story from Chapter 7. Consider reading or paraphrasing one or two other stories from the chapter as appropriate. For the annual award, prepare and read a story of the award recipient(s) during a faculty gathering, initially disguising the recipient(s)' identity and building anticipation by using the language "this teacher" or "this team" to narrate these relentless efforts and accomplishments. Gradually reveal the identity toward the end of the story with increasingly obvious hints, concluding with a standing ovation from the staff (much like the cheering stadium in the original improvement portrait). Consider featuring the award recipient(s) in the school newsletter or website. District leaders could also feature recipients across schools to broaden the impact and strengthen community appreciation for steady, persistent improvement efforts.

Team Exercise: After presenting the portrait, distribute copies of the six stories in Chapter 7 to all members of your leadership team or teacher team (see story files on the companion website). Ask participants to scan through the narratives and choose two stories to read. After reading both, choose one and write a paragraph about how the selected story might apply to your own work as a facilitator or leader of the instructional improvement process. Ask team members to share what they wrote with a partner. Then share several with the whole group, as time permits. (Download the "Courage and Persistence Reflection Exercise" from the companion website.)

Other Recommendations

• Spread out the introduction of portraits over time (one or two per year) to gradually deepen knowledge of improvement principles, develop shared language around key terms and concepts for inquiry, and renew faculty commitment for sustaining the process. Focusing on one portrait at a time allows for elaboration on the metaphor and key principle through steady application and deliberate teaching efforts across the year. This approach also extends the value and utility of the portraits over multiple years of implementation.

- Check the companion website for presentation slides (including digital images of the portraits) as well as individual copies of each metaphor description, slightly revised for generic use.

- Use the "Japanese Words and Audio" resources on the companion website for pronunciation help with *tsumayōji*, *kyōryoku*, and *ganbare*.

- After downloading the presentation notes and slides, create your own talking points by determining the length of your presentation or discussion and specific elements of the metaphor you want to emphasize.

- Also check the companion website for digital copies of the templates, tools, and checklists referenced in this guide, along with other helpful application resources and extension activities, including the "Protocol Criteria Checklist" (Chapter 3), the "Pilot Team Selection Inventory" (Chapter 3), the "Organizing Settings Template" (Chapter 5), and "Suggestions for Conducting Individual Inquiry With a Mentor" (Chapter 7).

- Develop your own presentation and application ideas for the portraits. Exchange ideas with your colleagues, and use #TeachingBetter on Twitter to share what you learn.

Application Outcomes

The images, stories, and resources in this book are specifically designed to help educators accomplish the following:

1. create a shared vision around key principles of continuous improvement and collaborative instructional inquiry;

2. deepen understanding of essential skills and mindsets required to engage in collaborative instructional inquiry;

3. establish a framework for supporting collaborative instructional inquiry across multiple teacher teams; and

4. find inspiration to persist with steady, systematic improvement over time.

Readers who make serious efforts to incorporate these ideas into practice should expect to see progress with the following indicators in their school communities or implementation contexts:

1. evidence of shared language and frequent references to the key principles of continuous improvement and collaborative inquiry (as described in the book);

2. gradual increase in the depth of discourse, tolerance for detailed planning, more fully articulated rationales for instructional choices, openness to learning from colleagues and alternative approaches, better use of evidence to substantiate analyses, more "we" language and emphasis on improving teaching rather than critiquing individual teachers;

3. more consistent, efficient, and effective assistance for teacher teams; greater bonds of trust between teachers and administrators; increased clarity and focus for instructional leadership roles and settings; tighter links between settings and role groups engaged in collaborative inquiry; and

4. increased resolve, commitment, and resilience for sustaining instructional improvement over time.

Visit the *Teaching Better* companion website at (http://www.corwin.com/ErmelingTeachingBetter).

Glossary

Japanese Words and Phrases

bansho	board writing
bansho keikaku	board-writing planning
beikoku kenshū	America study
ganbare	keep fighting; give it your all (stand firm; remain stubborn for a long time)
hansei	self-critical reflection
hansei kai	reflection meeting
jikkuri	steady, diligent, and tenacious approach to learning that places value on process and avoids setting close, easy goals
jiritsu	independence; self-reliance
jugyō kenkyū	lesson study
kanji	Chinese characters
katakana	Japanese alphabet used specifically for imported foreign words
kenkyū jugyō	research lesson
kikan shidō	between-desks instruction
kōkai kenkyū jugyō	public research lesson
kokuban kakari	person in charge of the chalkboard
kōnai kenkyū jugyō	within-school research lesson
kyōiku kenkyū kai	education research meeting (district level)
kyōryoku	collaboration (power is multiplied to the fullest extent when we work together productively)
neriage	polishing ideas through discussion

Osaki ni shitsurei shimasu	I am deeply sorry for being so rude as to leave before you.
Otsukaresama deshita	You must be very tired. Thank you for your hard work.
shokuin shitsu	staff room (or teachers' room)
tsumayōji	toothpick

Need Help With Pronunciation?
Visit the *Teaching Better* companion website for audio clips with pronunciation of each word (http://www.corwin.com/ErmelingTeachingBetter).

Index

Activity versus achievement, and instructional improvement difficulties, 89–90

Applications for collaborative instructional inquiry in U.S., 6–7

Assistance Matrix, and leadership through assistance, 116, *117–118*, 119–120

Basketball coaches' stories of courage and persistence
  Bias, 158–160
  Wooden, 157–160

"Best practices," and continuous instructional improvement, 87–90

Bias, Henry "Hank," and basketball coach's courage and persistence, 158–160

Campbell, D. T., 13

Chalkboards in Japan. *See also* Instructional improvement
  board writing or *bansho*, 15
  board-writing planning or *bansho keikaku*, 15
  person in charge of the chalkboard or *kokuban kakari*, 14

Challenge/rich problems or concept task, and instructional improvement difficulties, 87–88, 99

Coauthor inquiry narratives, and leadership through assistance, 116, *117–118*, 119–127

Cochran-Smith, M., 91

Collaboration, teacher. *See* Teacher collaboration

Collaborative inquiry case study in U.S.
  conclusions and, 80
  conditions for collaborative improvements and, 72–80
  facilitation of inquiry as condition for collaborative improvements and, 74–76
  hypotheses articulation and tests and, 57–59
  lesson contexts and, 57, *57*
  lesson revisions and, 65–71
  meeting summaries on results for research lessons and, 62–65, *63–64*, 68
  multi-semiotic modes and, 57
  observations and reflections on lessons as condition for collaborative improvements and, 78–80
  phases and time for project and, 55, *56*
  pilot project guidance and, 76
  practitioner resources and, 6
  protocols and, 77–78
  recursive process focused on improving teaching as condition for collaborative improvements and, 76–78
  reflection questions and, 80
  reflections on results for research lessons and, *64*, 65, *70*, 71–72
  research project and, 53–54, *54*
  research theme identification and, 55–57
  results for research lessons and, 59–65
  stable settings as condition for collaborative improvements and, 73–74
  struggle/scaffold script as storyline for lessons and, 58–59
  student inquiry changes and, 68, 71
  teacher inquiry changes and, 71
  teaching better and, 1
  "telling" to productive struggle shift and, 58
  toothpick or *tsumayōji* portrait and, *50*, 50–52, 79, 165–166
  transfer of knowledge and, 57–58
  video-based lesson observations and, 55, 62, *63–64*, 68, *69–70*, 78–80

Collaborative inquiry, 1–2, 44, 131, 170–171. *See also* Inquiry; Instructional improvement; Instructional improvement difficulties; Leadership, and assistance; Practitioners' stories of courage and persistence; Reviving problematic teams; Teacher collaboration studies; collaborative inquiry case study in U.S.; Teachers' culture

Collaborative inquiry teams, and U.S. schools, 131

Collective ownership, 43–44, 141, 170–171

Common ground story, and reviving problematic teams, 136–140, *139*

Communities of practice, and U.S. schools, 131

Concept task or rich/challenge problems, and instructional improvement difficulties, 87–88, 99

Conditions for collaborative improvements, and collaborative inquiry case study in U.S., 72–80

Council of Chief State School Officers, 1

Cultural teaching scripts, 1, 15

David, S., 107–108

Depth and quality of collaborative inquiry and lesson study in U.S., 2

Dewey, J., 93, 166

Digital libraries, and instructional improvement difficulties, 88, 92, *94*, 94–98, *95*, 99

Digital Promise League of Innovative Schools, 16

Ecological validity, and lesson study or *jugyō kenkyū* in Japan, 23–24

Effective practices, and instructional improvement difficulties, 89

Elmore, R., 109

Evidence-based findings
    instructional improvement difficulties and, 85–86
    lesson study or *jugyō kenkyū* in Japan and, 42–43

Expansive change difficulties. *See* Instructional improvement difficulties

Facilitation of inquiry, and conditions for collaborative improvements, 74–76

5000 reasons to quit portrait, *4, 146,* 146–148, 160, 169

Future Schools Promotion Project, 17

Gallimore, R., 11

Givvin, K., 99

Glossary of Japanese terms, 172–173

Ground rules for meetings, 141–142

Hiebert, J., 11, 15, 23–24, 91

Hurd, J., 78

Hypotheses articulation and tests
    collaborative inquiry case study in U.S., and, 57–59
    lesson study or *jugyō kenkyū* in Japan and, 41–42

Improvement portraits
    description of, 2–4, *3–4*
    5000 reasons to quit, *4, 146,* 146–148, 160, 169
    integration of portraits, principles, and stories, 4–6
    joint productive activity or JPA, *4,* 130, *130,* 131–132, 140, 168–169

key principles for each portrait, 3–4, 10, 18, 22, 46, 50, 80, 84, 102, 106, 128, 130, 144, 146, 161
    leader's guide to, 163–171
    recommendations for use of, 169–170
    rich drop of food coloring, *3, 22, 22,* 24, 45, 164–165
    rotting ship at sea, *3, 10,* 12–13, 17–18, 163–164
    toothpick or *tsumayōji, 3, 50,* 50–52, 79, 165–166
    virtual treasure chest, *3, 84, 84,* 93–94, 99, 166–167
    winter horseshoes, *3, 106,* 106–108, 113, 167–168

Individuals and specific teams strategies, 142–143

Inquiry, 13. *See also* Collaborative inquiry
    facilitation of inquiry as conditions for collaborative improvements, 74–76
    student inquiry changes in collaborative inquiry case study in U.S., 68, 71
    teacher inquiry changes in collaborative inquiry case study in U.S., 71

Inquiry teams, and U.S. schools, 131

Instructional improvement. *See also* Improvement portraits; Instructional improvement difficulties
    chalkboards in Japan and, 13–16
    collective ownership and, 43–44, 170–171
    conclusions and, 17–18
    cultural teaching scripts and, 15
    inquiry and, 13, 170–171
    intentionality and urgency balance and, 11–12
    reflection and, 13
    reflection questions and, 18
    rotting ship at sea portrait and, *10,* 12–13, 17–18, 163–164
    steady, diligent, and tenacious approach to learning that places value on process and avoids setting close, easy goals or *jikkuri* and, 17
    teacher collaboration studies and, 43–44, 85–86, 131
    teaching better and, 7
    technological devices and, 14, 16–17
    U.S. and Japanese approaches comparison and, 15, 16–17

Instructional improvement difficulties
    activity versus achievement and, 89–90
    "best practices" and, 87–90
    between-desks instruction or *kikan shidō* and, 96

conclusion and, 101
digital libraries and, 88, 92, *94,* 94–98,
    95, 99
effective practices and, 89
evidence of limitations in instructional
    improvement and, 85–86
knowledge access and, 91–92
knowledge defined and, 91
learning goals as uncoupled from
    instructional methods and, 88–89
pedagogical content knowledge or PCK
    and, 91
plug-and-play approach as discouraging
    continuous instructional
    improvement and, 87–88
polishing ideas through discussion or
    neriage and, 94–95
professional judgment development and,
    99–101
professional judgment development with
    live observations and, 100–101
professional judgment development with
    videos and, 100
professional knowledge expansion and,
    90–92, *94,* 94–99, *95*
reasons for, 86–87
reflection questions and, 102
reflective practice and, 86
rich/challenge problems or concept task
    and, 87–88, 99
teacher collaboration evidence and, 85
teaching through problem-solving or TTP
    and, 94, *94*
TIMSS classroom videos and, 88, *95,* 95–98
virtual treasure chest portrait and, 84, *84,*
    93–94, 99, 166–167
Intentionality and urgency balance, and
    instructional improvement, 11–12

Japan. *See also* Chalkboards in Japan
    glossary of Japanese terms, 172–173
    joint productive activity or JPA portrait
        and, *4,* 130, *130,* 131–132, 140,
        168–169
    teachers' culture in, 4, 30, 44–45, 52
    TIMSS classroom videos and, 15, *95,*
        95–98
    toothpick or *tsumayōji* portrait and,
        3, 50, 50–52, 79, 165–166

Kersting, N. B., 99, 100
Key principles for each portrait, 3–4, 10, 22,
    50, 84, 106, 130, 146
    reflection questions for each key principle,
        18, 46, 80, 102, 128, 144, 161

Knowledge
    instructional improvement difficulties
        and, 91
    knowledge access, 91–92
    leadership through assistance and, 121
    pedagogical content knowledge or
        PCK, 91
    professional knowledge expansion, 90–92,
        94, 94–99, *95*
    tacit knowledge, 121
    transfer of knowledge, 57–58

Leadership, and assistance
    Assistance Matrix, 116, *117–118,*
        119–120
    coauthor inquiry narratives and,
        116, *117–118,* 119–127
    conclusions and, 127–128
    improvement portraits guide and,
        163–171
    instructional support team or IST and,
        112–116, 119–124
    Knowledge about Teaching and
        Learning or KTL Summaries and,
        121–127, 168
    knowledge defined and, 121
    performance assistance, 109–110
    reflection questions and, 128
    settings organization and, 113–116, *114*
    tacit knowledge and, 121
    traditional patterns of assistance,
        108–109
    Triadic Model and, *110,* 110–113, *111,*
        112, 116
    winter horseshoes portrait and, *106,*
        106–108, 113, 167–168
Learning communities, and U.S. schools,
    44, 131
Learning Forward, 1, 174
Learning goals as uncoupled from
    instructional methods, and
    instructional improvement difficulties,
    88–89
Learning teams, and U.S. schools, 131
Lesson contexts, and collaborative inquiry
    case study in U.S., 57, *57*
Lesson revisions
    collaborative inquiry case study in U.S.
        and, 65–71
    lesson study or *jugyō kenkyū* in Japan and,
        30–36, *31–35*
Lesson study, and U.S. schools, 2, 131
Lewis, C., 78
Little, J. W., 86
Lytle, S., 91

Math teacher, and practitioner stories of
 courage and persistence, 154–157
Meetings
 ground rules and, 141–142
 reflection meetings or *hansei kai*, 30, 36,
  37–38, 41, 43
 summaries of results for collaborative
  inquiry case study in U.S. and,
  62–65, *63–64*, 68
Metaphors, improvement. *See* Improvement
 portraits
Mills College Lesson Study Group, 94, *94*
Mindsets and skills learned, and lesson study
 or *jugyō kenkyū* in Japan, 39–45
Multi-semiotic modes, 57

Napoleon, 107–108
National Commission on Teaching and
 America's Future, 1
Neurath, O., 12, 17. *See also* Rotting ship at
 sea portrait

Observations and reflections on lessons,
 and conditions for collaborative
 improvements, 78–80

Performance assistance, and leadership
 through assistance, 109–110
Persistence with problems over time, 44–45
Phases and time for projects
 collaborative inquiry case study in U.S.,
  55, *56*
 lesson study or *jugyō kenkyū* in Japan,
  25, *26*
Pilot project guidance, and collaborative
 inquiry case study in U.S., 76
Plug-and-play approach, and instructional
 improvement difficulties, 87–88
Portraits, improvement. *See* Improvement
 portraits
Practitioner resources, 6
Practitioners' stories of courage and
 persistence
 about, 148
 basketball Coach Bias and, 158–160
 basketball Coach Wooden and, 157–160
 Chinese characters or *kanji* and, 147
 English as a Second Language or ESL
  teacher and, 150–152
 5000 reasons to quit portrait and,
  146, 146–148, 160, 169
 keep fighting/give it your all or *ganbare*
  and, 147, 148
 math teacher and, 154–157
 reflection questions and, 161

science teacher and, 153–154
 special education teacher and, 149–150
Principles for reviving problematic teams,
 140–143
Productive action, and team improvements,
 133–136, 142
Professional judgment development
 instructional improvement difficulties and,
  99–101
 live observations and, 100–101
 videos and, 100
Professional knowledge expansion, and
 instructional improvement difficulties,
 90–92, *94*, 94–99, *95*
Professional learning communities, and U.S.
 schools, 1–2, 44
Project RED, 16
Project reflections
 lesson study or *jugyō kenkyū* in Japan and,
  38–39
 research lesson results in collaborative
  inquiry case study in U.S. and,
  64, 65, *70*, 71–72
Protocols for collaborative inquiry and lesson
 study, 6, 77–78

Recursive process, and conditions for
 collaborative improvements, 76–78
Research projects
 collaborative inquiry case study in U.S.
  53–54, 59–65
 lesson study or *jugyō kenkyū* in Japan,
  25–30
Research theme identification
 collaborative inquiry case study in U.S.
  and, 55–57
 lesson study or *jugyō kenkyū* in Japan
  and, 27
Reviving problematic teams
 Chinese characters or *kanji* and,
  131–132, *132*
 collaboration or *kyōryoku* and, 131–132,
  132, 140
 collective ownership of goals and, 141
 common ground story and, 136–140, *139*
 conclusion and, 143–144
 ground rules for meetings and, 141–142
 joint productive activity or JPA portrait
  and, 130, *130*, 131–132, 140,
  168–169
 learning communities described and, 131
 productive action and, 142
 reflection questions and, 144
 reviving problematic teams principles,
  140–143

shared goals and, 133, 135–136, 140–141
strategies for specific teams and
individuals and, 142–143
successful action story and, 133–136
target language or TL and, 138–139, 139
teacher collaboration described and, 131
Rich/challenge problems or concept task, and
instructional improvement difficulties,
87–88, 99
Rich drop of food coloring portrait, 3, 22, 22,
24, 45, 164–165
Rotting ship at sea portrait, 3, 10, 12–13,
17–18, 163–164

Science teacher, and practitioner stories of
courage and persistence, 153–154
Settings organization
leadership through assistance and,
113–116, 114
stable settings for collaborative
improvements and, 73–74
Shared goals, 133, 135–136, 140–141
Shulman, L. S., 91
Singer, T. W., 78
Skills and mindsets learned, and lesson study
or jugyō kenkyū in Japan, 39–45
Sotelo, F., 99
Special education teacher, and practitioner
stories of courage and persistence,
149–150
Specific teams and individuals strategies,
142–143
Stable settings, and conditions for
collaborative improvements, 73–74
Stigler, J., 11, 15, 23–24
Stigler, J. W., 99
Storyline for lessons
lesson study or jugyō kenkyū in Japan and,
40–41
struggle/scaffold script in collaborative
inquiry case study in U.S. and,
58–59
Strategies for specific teams and individuals,
142–143
Student inquiry changes, and collaborative
inquiry case study in U.S., 68, 71
Successes, and teacher collaboration
improvements, 133–136, 140–143

Tacit knowledge, 121
Teacher collaboration, and U.S. schools,
44, 131. See also Reviving problematic
teams

Teacher collaboration studies
collaborative inquiry and, 2
improvement difficulties and, 85–86
varied purpose and effectiveness and, 131
instructional improvement and, 13, 43–44
protocols and, 6, 77–78
Teacher inquiry changes, and collaborative
inquiry case study in U.S., 71
Teachers' culture
Japan, 4, 30, 44–45, 52
U.S., 1, 11–12, 44, 45, 52, 91
Teaching better, 1–2, 7, 170–171. See also
Collaborative inquiry; Collaborative
inquiry case study in U.S.; Instructional
improvement; Instructional
improvement difficulties; Leadership,
and assistance; Practitioners'
stories of courage and persistence;
Reviving problematic teams; Teacher
collaboration studies; Teachers' culture
Technological devices, 14, 16–17
"Telling" to productive struggle shift, and
collaborative inquiry case study in
U.S., 58
Traditional patterns of assistance, 108–109.
See also Leadership, and assistance
Transfer of knowledge, and collaborative
inquiry case study in U.S., 57–58
Triadic Model, and leadership through
assistance, 110, 110–113, 111,
112, 116

United States. See also Collaborative inquiry
case study in U.S.
Japanese and U.S. approaches comparison
and, 15, 16–17
teachers' culture in, 1, 11–12, 44, 45,
52, 91
technological devices and, 16–17
TIMSS classroom videos and, 15, 88

Video-based lesson observations, and
collaborative inquiry case study in U.S.,
55, 62, 63–64, 68, 69–70, 78–80
Virtual treasure chest portrait, 3, 84, 84,
93–94, 99, 166–167

Winter horseshoes portrait, 3, 106,
106–108, 113, 167–168
Wooden, John, and basketball coach's
courage and persistence, 157–160

Yoshida, M., 15–16

CORWIN
A SAGE Publishing Company

Helping educators make the greatest impact

CORWIN HAS ONE MISSION: to enhance education through intentional professional learning.

We build long-term relationships with our authors, educators, clients, and associations who partner with us to develop and continuously improve the best evidence-based practices that establish and support lifelong learning.

learningforward

THE PROFESSIONAL LEARNING ASSOCIATION

Learning Forward is a nonprofit, international membership association of learning educators committed to one vision in K–12 education: Excellent teaching and learning every day. To realize that vision, Learning Forward pursues its mission to build the capacity of leaders to establish and sustain highly effective professional learning. Information about membership, services, and products is available from www.learningforward.org.

Solutions you want. Experts you trust. Results you need.